SCREAMING FROM THE INSIDE

Incarcerated Women And The Journey To Awakening

Annala d'

Copyright © 2020 by Dream Catch Publishing

Published by Dream Catch Publishing

www.dreamcatchpublishing.com

ISBN 978-0-578-63768-6

Front and Back Cover Graphic Designed by **Terese Devries**

Soft Editing: **Jean Mobley**

Release Editor: **Eden Prosper**

All rights reserved. No part of this book may be reproduced, stored in a retrieval system, or transmitted in any form, by any means, including mechanical, electronic, photocopying, recording, or otherwise without prior written permission of the publisher.

Printed in the United States of America

About the Author

Annala d' is recognized as a powerful orator and teacher. She brings a unique ability to communicate life's challenges into moments of revelation. Her life path has brought her to an inflection point where standing idle in the presence of inequality and injustice is not an option.

Annala spent two years in the Georgia prison system. Unbelievably, she embraced this time and used it to her advantage. Achieving a deeper, more meaningful understanding of her true self and the power of waiting through the force of will, lead her to write 2 books that relate to her experience in prison and her emergence into freedom. She has since invested her time encouraging and standing with those who are most often impacted by our society's failings. She is a consistent voice for all those who go unheard.

Annala d' brings an unusual, yet practical perspectives to any endeavor, in addition to speaking and writing she is engaged with the business community. Through the visualization of what success looks like, she has helped many small businesses refine their strategies and ultimately achieve their goals.

Visit: http://www.dreamcatchpublishing.com for more info.

Stay tuned for other upcoming releases…

- **How To Prepare A Parole Package – Triggering Your Release From Prison**
- **Screaming From The Inside - Incarcerated Women And The Journey To Awakening**
- **Awaken On the Inside (Series)**
- **First Class Ticket – On the Mother Ship**

Dedication

Screaming From The Inside is dedicated to my children, **Timmesha, Jessica, Will, and his wife Icey**, my additional daughter, and **Cashina**, my firstborn. I am your mother, and I have learned so much from you. You encouraged, supported, and loved me when I did not believe I could go on another day. I can never repay you for everything that you have given, and what you continue to give.

The reader you will discover in this book that my release date was May 14th, which is the date of my youngest daughter, Timmesha's birthday. Because of this, my release date to mean so much as this means a double blessing.

Also, it would be amiss of me not to mention Thomas, who discovered me after my journey and now vibrates the energy that my heart and mind resonates with.

Dr. Joseph (Joe) Beasley, thank you for getting up early and attending court on my behalf. You did this more than once, and you did it despite being at the seasoned age of 80 plus. I want you to know that your love carried the energy that caused me not to stop fighting for my freedom. You are forever one of the most excellent mentors in my circle.

Thanks to every one of "YOU," those who knew me personally and those who knew me through my children. Thanks for writing letters and speaking up on my behalf, and thank you for contributing your financial resources to the cause to help me. There are too many of you to name on an individual basis, but you know who you are. I vibrate love and peace to each of you. You will always have a special place in my heart.

I also take this opportunity to thank the ladies at Pulaski State Prison for sharing and helping to guide me through this journey. You know who you are!

I Am One With All Within The Universe!

INTRODUCTION

Writing this book helped me to reshape the narrative that had been written ages ago about my ancestors and allowed me to transform pain into power. ***Screaming From The Inside*** is not your typical go-to prison book and learn about God. In this book, you will find yourself checking your moral compass, and then taking a careful look at the world that you have been creating.

You will laugh and cry, but beyond that, you will learn a vital truth at every turn. You will begin to realize that we are greater than the journey. Moreover, you will learn that within you lives a conqueror, and you are that conqueror.

Screaming From The Inside unpacks the knowledge that may allow you to release the power that is within us, but because of an untrained mind, we have allowed the illusions of this world to hide such power in the shadows. So, sit back, open your mind, and read about the journey that shifted pain into power for me.

It is my heartfelt desire that after you read this book, you will see from within. Then you too will "Scream From The Inside," as the Truth has always been present!

CONTENTS

Introduction --- vii

CHAPTER 1: Step Back ... The Last Day of a 3 Day Trial ------ 1

CHAPTER 2: The Chains of Capture ------------------------------- 5

CHAPTER 3: Joining Captives ... On the Local Plantation --- 11

CHAPTER 4: Reflection... The Set-up Contact ------------------ 14

CHAPTER 5: Meanwhile ... Back In Local Captivity... Anger Filled Room -- 18

CHAPTER 6: Reflection ... The Decision ... --------------------- 23

CHAPTER 7: Meanwhile ... Back In Local Captivity... The Visit ... The Struggle Within ... Thoughts to make the hurt end -- 27

CHAPTER 8: Reflection ...Universe Providing A Way of Escape... --- 34

CHAPTER 9: Meanwhile...Back In Captivity...Shifting Pain Into Power --- 49

CHAPTER 10: Reflecting... The Whisper of Fate... The Raging Storm Arrives...Sacrifice Led to Slaughter... ----------- 56

CHAPTER 11: Reflecting...The Trap Was Set...The Initial Capture was Formality... --- 65

CHAPTER 12: Meanwhile...Destination...Prison Slave Camp at Diagnostics...The Encounter...No More Reflecting -------- 79

CHAPTER 13: C-Hall OR Mental Ward...Survival OF The Fittest --- 87

CHAPTER 14: Killing Captives Softly With Meds ---------------- 95

CHAPTER 15: ...Making of the Mafia Environment ------------ 97

CHAPTER 16: Rehabilitation in Prison is the Illusion...A Trained Mind is the Solution -------------------------------------- 102

CHAPTER 17: The Awakening ----------------------------------- 104

CHAPTER 18: Trapped by the Villein...Released by Another --- 109

CHAPTER 19: Sold July 17, 2017, to the Highest Bidder...Pulaski State Prison -------------------------------------- 113

CHAPTER 20: Illusion of The Savior Attorney -------------------- 119

CHAPTER 21: Too Close for Comfort ---------------------------- 120

CHAPTER 22: Moving in the Flow of Prison Slave Camp... 124

CHAPTER 23: Dying to be Free -----------------------------------131

CHAPTER 24: Prison Camp/Mental Ward or Both ----------- 135

CHAPTER 25: US Constitution...Amendment 13 Dressed Up As Rehabilitation --- 138

CHAPTER 26: Ancestor Intervention-The Lessons ----------- 145

CHAPTER 27: Path to Least Resistance is Freeing ----------- 150

Chapter 1

Step Back
The Last Day of a 3 Day Trial

It is March 2017, and I was in the Superior Court in the City of LaGrange, State of Georgia. "Stand and face the judge," whispered my attorney. Whispering, I ask, "what is happening?"

Turning, he looked at me and in a hushed tone, he said: "The jury is back from deliberating and has reached a decision."

My physical body went into shock. "Back from deliberation? When did this happen?" I asked him.

"During lunch," he said with a frown, using the same hushed tone. For just a moment, my spiritual self detached from my physical body, and my spiritual person could see my physical body standing. My spiritual self looked around, an awareness or a knowing hovered over the room, then just like that, my mental and physical entities reunited. My physical body seemed to become numb immediately. Not because the atmosphere is cold, but because now, looking around the room, I was aware, for the first time, and had a real knowledge of what this sister of color was up against. The Faces of those sitting in judgment of me seem to become more vivid. I suddenly become aware that my attorney is white, and had been brown-nosing with the state prosecutors and the investigator during the three-day trial. The judge is white and had told me before I exercised my constitutional rights that he would be presiding over the case, and that he would move in the direction of the DA. The DA and all the DA's assistants are white and had already informed me of how they would influence the court and the jury of my guilt even as they offered me a plea. The jury consisted of three blacks who work in the community. These people of color work for the whites who control the town. The remainder of the jury are whites, and all of the State's witnesses are white, except for the co-defendant. At that moment, I understood what my spiritual self was alerting my physical person to, and my mind silently said, Girl! you have just been captured in a prison slave camp, and I **"Screamed from the Inside!"**

I decided at that moment that although I was screaming from the inside, I would not allow those who served injustice to witness me screaming on the outside. I willed my mind to think about my ancestors who not that long ago, were seized and taken into slavery, yet my ancestors remained mentally and physically strong. I thought about my children, who are strong because they are born from the seed of strength. They are the seed of my ancestors, and they have witnessed my power through many challenges. So at the moment when I was expected to break down and cry, I decided, *not now, not today, and not before those who are **unjust** would I break down*. I looked at the judge; I heard the guilty verdict from the jury. I hear the judge speak to me, but what did he say? I realize his lips are moving; my attorney speaks to me and interrupts my thoughts.

"The judge is asking if you wish to speak before sentencing," said the attorney.

I willed my mouth open, and words formed, and I spoke. ***"I did not do this judge; you did not hear my side; it was out of fear that I did not get on the stand,"*** I said. Reflecting on that moment in time, my attorney encouraged me not to take the stand. He said we could win without me getting on the stand. He said that the court would confuse everything, and I could get a lot of time if I took that position. So yes, I must admit fear was present, but yet I appeared strong in the midst of those who sought to oppress me. Perhaps this was the reason why the judge looked at me after I finished speaking and said, **"even now you don't have any remorse, this is a matter of public trust. I am sentencing you to 20 years in prison and 30 years of probation upon your release,"** he raised his gavel and hit the mark, and his judgment was hurled directly to me.

(On the inside, I am screaming, but those external from my thoughts cannot hear. My scream sounds only in my mind. This is wrong; I was not in a public trust position. I am the public who trusted. This is not justice, but I am voiceless. I feel helpless and powerless. Take her into custody, the judge said to the officer with the gun. I look around for someone to speak for me, for someone to say you can't do this to this wife, this mother, and grandmother, this business owner who has staff back at her office and clients who are depending on her, but there is no one.)

My family had not been present throughout the three-day trial, as I believed that justice would prevail for me in a court of law. I had advised my family that I would be ok. I knew that I was innocent, and even if the court would not, believe me, I thought I would get probation. After all, I had never been in any trouble. This charge was a non-violent offense. Never could I have imagined that a judge had the power to do such an evil thing as to sentence me to twenty years in prison. I try to search my attorney's face for answers, but he is pleading with the judge to allow us to present my witnesses after telling the judge that very same morning that we were not going to present any witnesses. He seemed to have sobered from whatever mental fog he was under during the trial, but his plea to the unjust judge receives a resounding "*No*."

Chapter 2

The Chains of Capture

I recognize the officer placing the cuffs on me. He was gentle. Perhaps he remembered me as I had previously worked with him at the City of Lagrange. My physical body wanted to cry a river of tears. My mind gave my physical body permission to cry, but the spiritual self within did not "Will" tears to be shed at that moment. My human self could not understand why I was not crying; had I already used all of my tears in my past challenges? Perhaps I am dreaming and will wake up. Thoughts rush through my mind as I am being ushered away and out of the court by the officer. I see faces looking at me as I am moving through the courtroom. I hold my head high as this was the only strength available to the human self. It was the strength of the spiritual nature within me that propelled my physical body forward. I was taken from the court and placed in what is called a holding cell. My entire body was still very numb. The tiny jail cell was freezing, was equipped with a hard cold cement bench. As I sat in the small cell alone, looking at the handcuffs that continued to hold my hands together, I could sense my mind and body thawing and now conscious of what looked like reality to the mind caused me to scream within.

I am so tired; I closed my eyes and fell asleep. Upon waking, the nightmare of being handcuffed in the tiny cell was still present. I opened my eyes to my attorney and his assistant, calling my name. As soon as I open my eyes, the attorney rushes to me. **"You know you can ask for parole right away. I am going to file for an appeal right away. You should participate in the choir if you go to Pulaski, I know the Warden there; this is not just a suggestion."** He concludes. My human self is looking at him, but my tongue seems to be frozen. I just stared at him, and thought, how could I have ever trusted you with my freedom? The scene reminded me of the movie, **12 YEARS A SLAVE**. In this movie, the main character believed the men who lied to him and sold him into slavery. I then turned my thoughts internally, turning to the real self as I had heard enough from the attorney who was supposed to represent me. I didn't recall the attorney and his assistant leaving, but when I refocused on my external surroundings, they were gone.

Shortly after the attorney and his assistant left, I had the knowledge or a knowing that I must fire that attorney. I hear the distinct jingling of keys, and another officer arrives. The officers take me from the holding cell, take me through what looks like an underground garage, and placed me in a vehicle designed to transport animals. I had to stoop very low to climb in the back of the vehicle, and I am 5'2. There were at least four other captives squeezed in the animal transport vehicle with me, and they were much taller. My keen sense of smell perceived the foul odor of recent animals that may have been transported in the same vehicle that was now being used to carry humans. I became nauseated. I closed my eyes and willed the feeling to subside. We were all taken to the jail on Sam Walker Drive. I would remain here, waiting to be transported to prison. The court concluded around 1:00 PM, but it was not until approximately 9:00 PM that evening I was permitted to make a phone call to my family as I was not allowed the phone call before I was processed in. I assumed the county jail wanted to make sure they were going to be compensated by the State of Georgia before they provided any services to their new captive.

(Make no mistake about it; this is how the game is played. It's about the money.)

Anyway, I know my family would be worried as they had not heard from me all day. I called my youngest daughter as her number was the only number that I had committed to memory. The phone rings, she answers quickly. I know she is anxious. I tell her what has happened, and just like her mother, she remains poised. **"We are only separated by a fence. Don't worry. We will fight for your freedom,"** she said.

I was allowed one phone call, so I asked my daughter to call my husband and the rest of the family to make them aware of my current status. We hung up after completing our conversation with promises to speak again.

After the phone call to my daughter ended, I was ushered back to Sam Walker Drive holding cell. This holding cell was larger, very cold and damp and consisted of a toilet area behind a partition wall. The single toilet served everyone in the tiny cell, and there was no escaping the waste odor. Privacy was now only a memory of a thing once treasured. When a captive used the toilet, others in the cell could observe the nakedness of the individual. I tried not to use the bathroom, but because I was held captive in this jail cell for many hours, nature demanded that I release it. As I watched the eyes of the captives gaze my uncovered body, I wanted to scream out, but I contained the tears behind my eyes.

The jail on Sam Walker Drive housed women and men in separate cells. Men were the only captives who were allowed to deliver food or perform details in or on the outside grounds of this county jail. I thought to myself, what an antiquated process; however, I didn't have the energy to be consumed with such thoughts at that moment. The entire jail at Sam Walker was more intimidating than the holding cell at the city jail as there were so many captives being held in cages, mostly black Americans. Most whites were processed in and out again. Waiting to be taken to the general population within the county jail seemed like forever. During my wait, one of the captured men became very agitated; he stripped off all his clothes, started hitting the glass windows of his cell, cursing and screaming. Fear raised its head within me. I thought the crazed man was going to break out and hurt everyone. I shut my alarm inside a compartment within myself and marked it, "no show today." For once, I was glad that I was behind a locked door. It was at this moment that I decided that I could choose to look at my current situation from a different perspective. Instead of feeling locked in, I decided that the locked doors existed to protect me from the things on the other side of the door. The agitated captive smeared feces over the glass door of the jail cell that retained him. Officers did not move to stop his behavior. The officers ignored him like his behavior was normal. I observed that the officers relocated the other captured men that were in the cell with the crazed man to a separate holding cell.

Finally, after about four hours, the seemingly crazed man quieted down. I was so sleepy. I had been getting up every morning at around 3:00 AM so I could travel back and forth to court for the last three days, and the drive was two and a half hours each way. Like a large boulder that had been rolling down a hill at a very high rate of speed, and had finally made an impact with the bottom, my body just wanted to rest. I found a spot around the ten other captives that were lying around on stone benches and on the floor in the cell. I finally Laid down and tried to rest, but my mind would not allow it, as fear was still on alert and peeking from within.

Finally, I was taken out of the holding cell and escorted to the showers. I was told to remove my clothes, bend over, and cough. This demand was hard for me. I was forced to allow a stranger to examine my body. As I was removing my clothes, tears began to rise to the surface of my pupils with a threat to break the barriers of my eye sockets for the first time since my sentencing. A strange feeling came over me. I felt as though the threatening tears wanting to make an appearance from my eyes had originated from a deeper part of me. They were not mine. They were not my tears. As I continued removing my clothes, I could sense the presence of my ancestors within me. I sensed their hurt as a result of what I was experiencing at that very moment. The pain I was experiencing seemed to be a shared experience with those who traveled this path before me. Growing up in the State of North Carolina, I heard stories of slavery but had not experienced it, nor did I have knowledge of my ancient ancestors. However, I could sense someone within my presence that I have no knowledge of. Yet, they were there. They were directing me and going through this experience with me. This sense of knowing provided me the power to back away the tears as my ancestors had done long ago, lift my head, and move beyond this point in time.

The shower looked like a scene from a movie of a third world country. It was past filthy and stained with mold and mildew clinging to the walls. I wanted to bleach the entire shower stall before I stepped one foot into it. I was happy to be provided with the worn shower shoes that looked like mold themselves. At least I did not have to place my feet on the filthy shower floor. There were no other options. I could use the dirty and filthy shower or not. I chose to bathe. After completing my shower, garments were provided to me that were faded out black and white striped elastic pants and a matching pullover top. The garments had the appearance of having been worn by many other captives before me. At least the clothes were clean, I thought to myself. Upon dressing, a thin bed mat, toiletries, and a worn blanket were provided to me, all of which I had to carry for what seemed like two blocks to where I would be housed for the next 30 to 45 days awaiting to be transported to the State prison.

Chapter 3

Joining Captives
On the Local Plantation

At approximately 11:00 PM, the officer is walking me to the cell housing, the general population of captives opens the locked door to what is called a POD. A POD is a huge open dorm room that holds approximately 120 women. Black iron like bunk beds is lined against two sides of the long gray, dingy walls. Natural finished looking wooden picnic tables are staggered throughout the center of the enormous room. There are windows along the top of the tall ceiling; a ceiling so high a person would need a cherry picker to view outside, and set so high that one would not be tempted to climb on a perch to catch a view of the sun from which the rays of light streamed. The tall windows were a reminder to every captive that the sun still rises and sets, but that you are now being held in captivity; therefore, "you" captives are not allowed to feel the splendor of the sun rays against your skin.

(I understood right away that the windows in this room existed only to allow the natural light to peek in, and never meant for those captured to enjoy the reality of the naturalness of the outside view.)

The dampness of the vast room attacks my nostrils. The place reeks of mildew. The walls are dingy and stained with mold, and leftover food particles are part of the flooring. "Find yourself a bunk," said the officer as she turns and leaves me on my own. There are so many women in the room; the noise level is so high that you could barely hear your thoughts. I walked in and stood, not sure of what to do or which bunk can carry the heavy load that I had struggled to bring.

"You are a cute little Mama. Let me help you with your bed," said the toothless girl smiling at me. I swear, I thought that I was looking at a female version of the joker as it relates to her physical body. Green hair is sticking up on the top of her head. She wore a very tight full-body Long Johns that were stained and dingy. They were perhaps white at one time. She has skinny legs and a huge upper body. Her lips were decorated with very red lipstick, and she had a smile that seemed to be turned upside down. I looked closely at her as I thought she might have been wearing a lip mask. Her lips were moving, and they were attached to her face! I wasn't sure if I should run or scream for help.

I managed to say, "no, thank you. I got it." I kept walking as I decided that setting up my temporary stay anywhere near this girl and her friends would not be good.

Laughing very loud, "she doesn't like you," said another girl.

"Fu-- you," said the girl with the green spiked hair. I heard their exchange of words as I continued walking and looking for a bunk in an area that I would feel safer.

I walked to the end of the long row of bunks looking left and right before I located an open bunk that my spirit agreed with. It was a top bunk, and the area seemed quieter. There was a young girl in the bottom bunk. "You want me to take the top bunk," she asked.

"No, thank you," I said.

"You want me to make up your bed for you?" she asked.

"No, thank you, I got it," I said. I just wanted to be left alone, and she did just that. I managed to get the mat on the bunk halfway, made up the bed, laid down without getting undressed, and drifted off to sleep even amid the loud voices speaking profanity. When I awakened, it was around 2:00 AM. There were a few people still awake playing cards. Looking around the room, I realized that the nightmare was still with me. I closed my eyes, reflecting on the past, trying to determine how my past leads me to such a tremulous present. With eyes shut, I go within, searching for answers in my past.

Chapter 4

Reflection – The Set-up Contact

"Hey, how are you?" spoke an unfamiliar voice, in a room filled with idle chatter. I look up from the nail carousel that served to dry polished nails and toes of the patron who wanted a quicker method of drying. I did not recognize any of the faces, so I assumed the hello was not for me. The carousel seated four individuals. I look down at the feet of those sitting around the carousel and notice the beautiful painted nails and toes of other women sitting at the drying station. I hear someone say "hello," again. I did not respond as I did not know anyone in this nail shop and assumed that the voice was not speaking to me. I hear the voice speak again, "hello."

I look around before I responded and meet a very friendly smile. A set of pleasant eyes of a well-dressed female was looking at me. Understanding that the voice is speaking directly to me, I finally responded, "hello." "Hello, how are you?"

The unfamiliar voice replies, "girl, just trying to do me."

"I understand that," I say in response to the woman. "I am Liza," said the woman.

"I am Ann," I said, introducing myself but not offering my last name.

"Do you work around here?" she asked.

"I work full time for the City of LaGrange, but I also operate a small business that assists in developing other small businesses. I plan to move into business full-time for myself very soon.", I said.

"I work full-time for Family and Children Services, but I do hair in my spare time," she said.

I looked at her as I am thinking to myself; how bad my hair must look. "I guess you can see that I am having a bad hair day," I said as I smiled.

She smiled and said, "I believe I can help you with that."

"Can you work with weaves?" I ask her.

"Yes, weaves are my specialty, and my services are performed out of the privacy of my home," she said with a smile.

"I may take you up on that," I said and adding, "I guess you can see my hair is a mess, but I need someone who can provide good work as I like believable weaves."

She laughed out loud, "I can make you brand new and believable," she said.

We both laughed, and then dived into small talk about our past experiences with hair salons.

"Are you ready to go," said two other well dressed and professional-looking women as they approached the woman who I had just met and who I now know as Liza. Liza responded, "in a moment."

One of the women spoke and said, "you know we are on our lunch hour, and we are already late."

"Don't worry about it, you are with your boss," Liza said.

"Well, I'm going to pay my bill," said one of the women as she moved toward the cashier attendant.

"This is on me, my treat," said Liza to the women.

Both women stopped and smiled, "are you sure," they said in unison.

"If I weren't sure, I would not have offered," said Liza.

They both said, "thank you. We will wait for you at the front."

As they began walking to the front, one of the women spoke words to the attendant, and they both sat down to wait for Liza.

Speaking to Liza, again, "it's great to be the boss," I said while smiling.

"Yes, it is," she said while examining the work performed on her nails and feet, touching them to ensure that they were dry, "but I guess I should get back." Seeming satisfied that both feet and nails were dry, she pulled out her wallet, looked at me, and smiled, "I hope to hear from you," she said. She stood up, walked away, approached the counter, and paid the attendant. She seems like a nice person; I thought to myself as treating someone to a "Me Day" is something that I would do.

(*Things are not always as they seem, please believe this.*)

Chapter 5

Meanwhile Back In Local Captivity
The Anger Filled Room

"Bit--, don't make me stomp your a--," my thoughts are interrupted by individuals being very loud and aggressive and using profanity. "Fu-- you, don't think you can pull that shi- on me." I hear voices booming in the room as likened unto the sound of continuous roaring thunder. Something hits and scrapes against the floor, voices escalate, my hands move, I pull the covers over my head. I feel myself trembling. I think to myself, and there is no door that secures me from the anger in this room. I remember being five years old again. My granny was arguing with her son. Her favorite flowers were being thrown to the floor by her son. This was a feeling and memory that I thought had dissipated long ago, but fear raised its cruel head, and just like then, I put my head under the covers. I told myself, relax, and breathe. All is well. I thought to myself, one more thing to add to my already filled plate; unwanted memories, but this too shall pass. Then, I hear a voice of authority! "Put the cards away, and go to bed now," said an on-duty officer. Angry voices mumble, but I hear feet walking away. Yet, my head remains hidden under the safety of the mildewed smelly blanket.

"Hot! I am so hot! I can't breathe!" I awaken with my head still under the blanket. My entire body is wet from sweat. My head peeks out from under the cover, and my eyes notice that it is daylight.

"Traaaaaa, traaaaaa, traaaaaa," someone screams.

I feel nervous. I have no idea what that term means, I think to myself. Is this a riot?

The girl on the bottom bunk stands up and addresses me. "Do you want your tray? My name is Lus, don't you want your tray?" she says again.

Her face looks young. She appears to be around 19 or 20. Her skin lacks luster, and she seems to suffer from malnutrition. Her eyes are sad, and she is wearing a headscarf that appeared to have been torn from a bedsheet, which is in dire need of being washed. My gaze must have seemed to her like a deer looking into headlights.

"Don't you want your tray?" she said again, leaning closer to me as if I suffered from deafness. "You better come on," she said nicely. "What's your name," she said.

"Ann," I stated as I climbed down from the upper bunk, still wearing the same clothes I slept in. I followed Lus to the line that ended at an exit door where the food trays were being shoved through.

"You gotta get in alphabetical order," said someone. I look around, trying to determine where the voice is coming from. I finally look down. The voice is booming from an individual that must weigh every bit of 250 pounds, is about four feet tall with beady eyes surrounded with blue eye shadow, and she was not smiling. The tiny person said again, "got to get in order. "What is your name?" she shouted.

I started to speak, and then Lus looking at me, saw my confusion and said, "what is your last name Ms. Ann?"

I told her, and then she directed me where to stand. Just in time, too, because the tiny person remarked, "hope she doesn't think she's getting in front of me."

I said to myself, "remember the person in front of you, Ann so you will know where to stand the next time." What I didn't know is that everyone was not in line, and other captives are brought in during the night. So remembering the person in front of me was not the solution to that challenge. I watched as the food trays were being shoved into the hands of the captured individuals as they proceeded through the line. It was then that I realized that the screaming person earlier this morning was referring to "tray," but what came out of their mouth was "traaaaaa." I almost smiled to myself. My turn finally came. My tray was shoved into my hand. A food product leaking from the tray caused my hand to become immediately moist. Tears rose in my eyes like they had been hiding out waiting to make their appearance, but again I willed the tears to stand down. With the tray in my hand, I had a glimpse of what being captured into this legal slave system is going to be like. I will be given the food that my captors want me to eat. Wear the clothes that they give me to wear, do what they tell me to do. As I sat down with my tray at one of the picnic tables, I realized that I could choose. No one can make me consume the awful smelling food being served in the disgusting dirty tray.

As I started to stand to take my tray to the discarded tray area where everyone else is taking their tray, I hear a voice, "you don't want your food?" I look up. I am shocked to see the woman who looked like the joker.

"No," I said. My tray was snatched quicker than a rat can grab cheese from a trap. I thought to myself that food is spoiled, she must be really hungry.

I wanted a shower. I asked Lus who was seated nearby where are the showers. She gave me the not so grand tour after she had finished her breakfast. The showers had four shower bays without any doors or curtains. The walls were engrained with mold and mildew stains. There was food on the shower floor and other trash particles. I was told that because the water gets hotter in the shower, the captives use the hot water in the shower to heat food such as noodles, and sometimes food is spilled on the floor. It did not make sense to me that they wouldn't pick up the mess, but I did not say anything about that. I thought to myself, I will take showers when the area is empty. As the tour continued, I noticed that the on and off switch for the showers would stay on for less than a minute, and then you had to push the button again to have the water start again. If you wanted really hot water, a person screams for someone in the toilet area, which was located a few feet away to flush the toilets continuously. This was the process of obtaining warm or sometimes hot water to take a shower or get hot water to heat food. The one bathroom was open. There were no entry or stall doors. Remembering my thoughts of no privacy hit home again. Although I could take a shower alone, this was not going to work for using the restroom. An individual became an open book in the bathroom. One can only imagine the humiliation that every woman faced when using the bathroom. This humiliation did not stop even with changing one's sanitary napkins or anything else. Captives would stand in the area and conversate while you were using the restroom. I got up early so that I could use the bathroom before others were awake, but someone was always there.

I realized I was not the only woman trying to hold what should be done naturally. There were other women who had never been in a jail cell and were not comfortable using the bathroom in front of others. There were those born as women, and there were those who had chosen an alternative lifestyle; however, those of us who decided womanhood were forced to use the restroom with those who chose manhood lifestyles.

(Don't misunderstand me. There is no bias in my statement. It is an observation and a truth.)

I did not realize I was quickly slipping into depression. I didn't eat for four days. Each day I gave my food to the quickest snatcher. I made sure no one was in the shower as I took my showers. I tried to use the bathroom when everyone else was asleep. When I talked to my family, I made them think I was ok. I slept or laid awake and continued thinking of the past that led to this present nightmare ...

Chapter 6

Reflection
The Decision

Looking into the mirror at my hair that is now screaming, "fix me," I thought to myself, I do not want to drive all the way to Atlanta from LaGrange to have my hair done. I had been driving to Atlanta for a while since I could not locate anyone in LaGrange who was familiar with the method of how I liked my hair. I thought about the offer of Liza and remembered that I have her business card. I sensed a thought-vibration within my inner self, "Don't call her." The vibration was as a gentle breeze, a subtle steering that brushed against my mind. The nudge of the vibration was so gentle that I ignored it. My personal-self became absorbed with what the physical body would look like with a new hairdo. My mind provided the stimulation necessary for my personal-self to make the final decision as it pointed out to my eyes how good my physical self would look with a new hairdo, and just like that, I dismissed the vibration of guidance. I picked up the phone and dialed. Liza answers the phone. Introducing myself, I said, "Hello, this is Ann, the woman with the bad hair day. We met in the nail shop on Commerce Drive in LaGrange." In a matter of minutes, I had arranged to travel to the home of Liza to have my hair done on a Friday evening after work. This was one week after I had met Liza at the nail shop.

Following the directions Liza provided, I arrived at her home with ease. I drove up a very steep driveway surrounded by a beautifully landscaped deep green lawn and an array of flowers adorned in many bright springtime colors. Finally, I was saluted by a two-story home that stood like the queen of its beautiful surroundings. I was impressed as I followed the wrap-around driveway to the back of the house as Liza's directions had dictated. I again sensed what I thought was indecision. Looking back now, I realize I was being provided a logical means of escape. Why don't you wait to get your hair done? I sensed the vibration within me again. I have never been known for patience, so waiting was not a solution that appealed to me. I again dismissed the feeling. I shut off my vehicle and exited my car. Liza opened the door before I could ring the doorbell. I said, "Hello, Ms. Liza" before she could speak. She stood there as if she was not going to invite me in. I thought, did I get the date wrong?

Then she smiled and said, "the password to get you in the door and get your hair done is using my first name without the Ms."

I smiled and agreed. I enter a beautifully decorated home that was just as well maintained as the landscaped lawn, and I expressed this to her. "Thank you. I try. What would you like to drink?" she said.

"Water is fine," I said.

We are seated in her kitchen. She retrieves a glass from the cabinet, fills it with water from the refrigerator, and hands it to me. "Let's chat a bit before we get started," she suggested.

We talked a lot, but now as I think back, we mostly talked about me and what I wanted. I spoke about my business and me as a business development consultant. We also talked about my work with the City of LaGrange. I liked talking about my business aspirations. Liza told me she was a children's counselor, and she had earned her Master's Degree in Counseling. She said that she worked for the Department of Family and Children Services. She also said that her Mom is a minister and that they moved from North Carolina by way of New York. She talked about the loss of her father, who had been very wealthy. We then talked about music as I had already mentioned to her that my daughter was interested in singing and modeling. She told me that she played a character once on a top-rated television show and that she was nominated for a musical award. She allowed me to see an album cover she was featured on and showed me photographs of her with a major song artist. I was impressed with Liza and said as much to her. Because my youngest daughter aspired to model, sing, and act, I believed that Liza could assist my daughter with her vision. My mind convinced my personal-self that Liza was divinely placed in my path.

Our conversations led to her talking about her special needs' daughter, who was spending time in North Carolina with her father and her son, who Liza defined as a bit of a challenge. I also talked about my husband, Stephen, who at this time was an over the road logistics driver. It was for this reason that I explained to Liza that we needed someone to provide lawn services as my husband was often on the road, and was very tired when he would arrive at home.

"Your lawn is so beautiful. Who performs your work?"

"My cousin," she said.

"If you don't mind, would you please have your cousin contact my husband as he is on the road driving a lot, and we need someone to take care of our yard," I said to her. She agreed to have her cousin contact us. Thank you so much. If I am not too pushy it would thrill and motivate my daughter if she could speak to you about the music industry. Would it be ok if I had her contact you?"

Smiling, she said, "yes, have her call me. A lot of people in the music industry don't want to help others who are trying to make it; I am not one of them," she said.

She finished up my hair, which took about three and a half hours. After looking in the mirror at my hair and discovering that I was not pleased with her work, I thought to myself, was this worth it? I paid and tipped her anyway as I imagined that she would be an asset to my daughter's musical ambitions, as well as the resolution to my family's yard maintenance challenge. Also, I thought she was someone worth getting to know. Driving back home and smiling to myself, I anticipated telling my baby girl the news I had discovered. I believed this would benefit my baby girl. Life seemed to be answering my prayers.

(I now understand that we must be aware that sometimes wolves wear sheep's clothing.)

CHAPTER 7

Meanwhile
Back In Local Captivity
The Visit
The Struggle Within
Thoughts to make the Hurt End

"Ms. Ann, you have to eat. They are going to put you on suicide lockdown if you don't eat for three days," said Lus.

"I will try," I said to Lus.

"Lus!" What's that new lady's name," screamed a captive from across the room.

"Her name is Ms. Ann," said Lus.

"Tell her she has a video visit," said the captive.

I was shown how to log in for my upcoming video visit with my daughter by Lus. My daughter appeared on the video screen; I hid the sadness behind a smile as I was genuinely happy to see a familiar face. We discussed closing my office in which I operated my business, issuing final payroll checks to my now unemployed staff, and closing my bank account. I asked if she had spoken with my husband about many other essential matters that my family was currently dealing with as a result of me being captured in the prison slave system. It was almost like I was preparing for death. I can only imagine if one could experience the taste of death while yet still alive. Would it feel like being captured, in the Georgia Slave Prison System?

I noticed my daughter studying me as she often does, trying to read my persona. "You look so frail, Mom. Are you eating?" she asked.

"I am trying," I said to her and added, "the food is not very pleasing to the eyes, and the trays are hard plastic and filthy."

"I am putting money on your books. I know you can't eat that food in there. Buy some food to eat," she said as we concluded our thirty-minute video visit. Buying food from the on-line store was very expensive, but it allowed me to regain my strength so that I could think.

There were so many things to think about, my family who needed me, clients who were depending on me, who had trusted and relied on me to manage their trucking companies, my community, and church family who trusted and respected me. As I reflect on those who I did not have an opportunity to realign resources for, tears again threaten my eye gates as I would never hurt anyone with intent, but I must keep writing my truth, I tell myself. Perhaps, one day, soon enough, I can speak and tell them that I am sorry that the effect of my hurt spilled over into their lives and caused them to hurt.

I was continually strengthened by my children, who took my phone calls and came to visit me. They nurtured my personal-self, encouraged my body not to give up, and helped me will my mind to think good thoughts. With this renewed strength, I called my husband, whom I had married after the death of my late husband, Stephen, in 2011. It is now 2017, and "My husband at the time," and I would have been married five (5) years on April 22. I think to myself, why am I afraid to call him? He is my husband for better or worse. I used the money that my daughter placed on my books to call him. "Hello," I said to my husband. "Hey Ann," he said with a tone that was not compassionate. I immediately understood why I delayed in calling him. His support was limited to non-existence during my trial. Now his tone portrayed my current standing in his life. I still prayed that our marriage would survive the storm, but felt my husband would desert me when the waves covered the shore of what he perceived was our happy home.

"Are you going to stand with me, honey?" Are you still in love with me," I ask my husband.

"I don't know," he said. "This is too much. The newspapers made you look terrible. I got a copy of the article," he said.

"You know me, you know I would not do the things I was accused of," I told him. I continued talking, "you don't love me anymore?" I ask.

"Yea, I loved you, but I can't say that I am in love with you anymore because you are not here," he said.

My heartfelt like someone turned off the valve that pumped blood into it. "I am going to let you go," I said to him and hang up the phone. I did not want the crowd of captives who hung around the area, watching television to witness my stress or my clouded eyes as tears were threatening to flow. As I walked away from the phone, *I Screamed from the Inside!*

My once renewed strength now seemed like a puddle of dissolved weakness topped with fear. I felt so alone. I had my children, but I also wanted the man who said he would love me for better or worse. I realized just where I'm placed in his life when he told me, "I didn't sign up for this." I thought to myself, just when I needed my husband the most, he abandoned me, and his abandonment felt like a kick in my face when I was already down. When I asked him to put $40.00 on my books, he said, "I need to pay these bills." Every time I called him I would end the call feeling worse. The church that I served and paid tithes to every week forgot about me. Some of my associates and those whom I defined as friends disassociated themselves from me. I wanted to end my life. No longer did I want to have faith and try to be strong. I had decided that the next person who said to me that "this too will pass," I was going to slap the words right back into their mouth. I thought to myself, how can I end this state of existence? I looked around for sharp objects that would assist me in reaching the goal of ending what I perceived as pain in my heart.

There was a room in the Sam Walker jail facilities referred to as a recreational room. It was designed like the room that held the bunk beds and captives, except it was completely empty and much smaller. I entered this room to be alone. I was elated to discover the place empty, as this was the hangout room for those who declared their love for each other. I was looking around on the floor, looking for nails that may be protruding from the walls, looking for something, anything that would help me to end my life on this plane of existence. I started walking around the room looking, and then I looked up at the small windows at the top of the room, trying to see the sky so I could scream at who I knew then, as God. The abated tears that had continued to threaten to show themselves rushed from their hiding place, dashing through the windows of my eyes like a waterfall. Just like a dam that was finally opened to release the water, the flood came. This time, there was nothing I could do to stop it, and I didn't want to.

My ears hear something, what is it? I try to gather my thoughts, try to listen to it again. "It's time for you to go back in," an authoritative voice shouted. My eyes try to focus. I think to myself, am I dreaming? Was I successful in taking my life, or did I fall asleep? I'm trying to figure out where I am. I wasn't supposed to wake up again in this place. Did I even attempt to end my life? When did I sit down? I am trying to figure it out. I think to myself; this was my day, my day to end this suffering! I'm trying to understand what happened. How did I end up sitting on the floor in a lotus position asleep? Raising his voice, "let's go!" repeated the officer. I got up, my legs are stiff, and my feet are still asleep. I'm still trying to understand. I walked back into a room filled with noise and confusion.

I decide to lay across the bunk assigned to me, and after some time, I apparently fall asleep. I am awakened by people screaming, using profanity, and fighting each other. My vision is blurred as I ascertained if I am perhaps dreaming. As I focus my eyes on the scene before me. All I could see were feet kicking and arms swinging. Captives were in the center of the room fighting like they were putting on a show, and those of us watching from the sidelines were paying spectators. Everything seems to be moving in slow motion through my sense of sight. Suddenly a red wig zooms across the room and lands right in front of the bunk I'm in. The girl with green hair, and wearing the same one-piece tight thermal suit, I refer to as Joker, has another captive in a chokehold. The tiny person who I now refer to as "Tiny" is biting the Joker on the leg. A new girl had arrived whose body was so vast that in my mind, I imagined that she had escaped from the land of the giants. I had never seen this girl before, but there she was, trying to pull Tiny from the leg of the Joker.

I closed my eyes and placed my hands over my ears. I do not want to hear or be a witness to this mayhem. I opened my eyes just when the door to the dorm blasts open. In trots, five officers dressed like swat. "Break it up," they scream, but the fighting captives are not listening. They continued to fight. I don't even think they realize the officers had entered the room. From what I could ascertain, the majority of the captives in the dorm were fighting. Lus stands up, looks at me from the bottom bunk. "Don't move Ms. Ann, just stay where you are," she stated.

"What makes you think I would move?" I thought to myself, but the words refused to move from my mind to my mouth. I only shook my head to indicate I understood her.

The officers finally bring order to the room. "What's this all about," stated one of the officers. "Bit-- stole my toilet paper and noodles," said Joker.

After restoring order and taking inventory of the wounded, the officers carry a girl out on a stretcher whose eyes were swollen badly, and she was bleeding. I suppose it was this girl who owned the red wig. I heard her mumbling as they were carrying her out, "shi-, get me my wig." An officer wearing a pair of gloves retrieves the red wig that had seen better days from the floor. He throws it on top of the beaten girl, and they roll the red wig and the wounded girl out of the dorm. Every captive in the fight was taken to lockdown but then was back the next day except for the beaten girl with the red wig. I thought to myself, oh boy, here we go again, but when the fighting captives returned, they were all talking and laughing together, like nothing ever happened.

(*I thought to myself, just like family, but not.*)

Understanding that those individuals were fighting about noodles and toilet paper caused me to think about someone other than myself. I thought it is a sad day when people would fight about something so simple. Witnessing the lack of captives having their human needs meet, brought tears to my eyes. This time the tears were for someone other than myself. I thought hard about the fight and what the fight was about, but before I could overthink about the jail scene, I had to reach deep within myself again. I needed to understand; how did my path lead me here…?!

CHAPTER 8

Reflection
Universe Providing A Way of Escape

I made it home after leaving Liza's house. My daughter, who at the time attended LaGrange College, is asleep. I decide to tell her the good news the next day.

"Are you serious mom?" asked my daughter when I tell her about Liza and her connections to the music industry.

"Let's call her right away," she says eagerly. "No, let's wait until after twelve, she may still be asleep," I say to my daughter.

My daughter must have watched the clock. "Mom, it is past noon," she said.

"Ok, let's call," I tell her. I am so excited. My daughter is talking to Liza, but when she hangs up the phone, she does not seem to be excited, and that's because she wasn't.

"What did she say," I asked?"

"A lot of things, but mostly that people that are in the business don't like to help others become successful. They think their glory will be stolen, but she said that she would try to help me," said my daughter.

"I am surprised, baby," I told her. "She talked like she had the connections to help and wanted to help you," I said. A vibration of thought flowed to my mind. Things are not as they seem. I ignored the subtle message again. Liza promised my daughter that she would be in contact.

I didn't see or hear from Liza for more than 8 months. By the time I heard from her again, I had resigned from the City of LaGrange and had started my business of DocQments fulltime. In addition, Liza's cousin had never called my husband Stephen about our lawn maintenance, and because I was extremely busy with my business and work, I dismissed meeting Liza. She was now a memory in my past.

(It's funny how your path looks so much clearer when you stop and pay attention to the road signs on the way. I must admit, this is something I never did. I was too busy trying to become successful and placing myself in the path of people who I thought could help me reach my destination.)

Before resigning from the City of LaGrange to operate my business fulltime, I proposed to the City of LaGrange management that I should be allowed under my capacity as a Business License Administrator to mentor individuals who were mandated to perform community services. These individuals had been charged with fines and interest that were incurred on their balances. The majority of individuals could not pay because of being financially disadvantaged.

Allowing the individuals to perform community services acted as compensation and reduced their fines. Being allowed to perform community services as a way to reduce one's fine was important to me as I had listened to individuals who would talk about their inability to pay the hefty fines and interest ordered upon them by the City of LaGrange legal system; Judges; and, District Attorneys. Most of these individuals were people of color and financially disadvantaged.

As I looked back over my existence on this earth, I realized that I have always been an advocate for the disadvantaged. My desire to advocate for those who were disenfranchised was awakened because of the manner in which my grandmother was treated. As a child living in North Carolina and witnessing the ill-treatment of my granny by those who in their mind perceived themselves as more advantaged because of their skin color caused me to want to change that picture.

(My endeavor for success has always been fueled by a deep desire to produce the substance necessary to become a better advocate for the disenfranchised and disadvantaged. I now understand that the root cause of my passion grew from a place deep within that received its nutrition from me growing up as a child of color in rural North Carolina and witnessing many people of color being taken advantage of.)

The Management agreed to establish the mentor community work program in our office. One of the individuals in the community mentoring program who had been assigned to work with me to complete community service was named Paula. She worked really hard and was also interested in starting a business. I was operating my business from my home while still employed with the City of LaGrange at the time, and my market was beginning to grow. I wanted to move into an office space as I began to feel uncomfortable with clients coming to my home. After Paula completed her community services, she contacted me.

"I have a place to operate your business if you are still interested and want to share the space," she said.

"I will come and see the place," I told her. Again, my thoughts tell me not to see Paula, but as soon as time permits, I traveled to Miller street in LaGrange to look at the office space. The building was rooted amid a very low-income neighborhood. The place on Miller Street looked desolate, but I am also one who believed in divine intervention. Even as I had undesired thoughts about the space, in my mind, I thought that everything would be worked out by God. Reflecting, I can still remember my intuitive mind nudging me, "don't do this," find another place. Fear raised its head, I gave it attention, and fear spoke; you can't afford the rent in another place by yourself. You know how high rent is, plus electric and water. You will be closing just as fast as you opened, said fear. I agreed with fear and decided to share the building with Paula.

The arrangement with Paula was not working out well. Our personalities and characters were miles apart, but because my business was starting to blossom, I stayed. One morning, Paula told me she was going to open another location in Newnan with another individual. When the individual came to the office to meet Paula, to my surprise, it was Liza. I thought to myself. It's a small world.

(I now understand that trouble has a way of seeking you out even if your attention to it is subtle.)

"Hello. How have you been," said Liza.

"Great," I said. We exchanged small talk; I learn that Liza is no longer employed with the Department of Family and Children Services. I thought to myself; she must have decided to go into business for herself.

Paula mentions that the person performing work on the lawn is Liza's cousin. I look out the window and see the man working on the lawn. Liza introduces me to her cousin, and I give him my husband's number to make arrangements to perform our lawn work. I also learn that Paula and Liza's cousin is in a relationship. Liza's cousin lives in LaGrange. Then I hear that Liza is moving from Newnan to LaGrange because her son was busted with drugs in her home, and she lost her home as a result. Liza discussed the events of her life openly, and I had sympathy for her. I had empathy for her as a mother trying to do the best she could, but it seemed like everything was against her. I understood because I had been there before. I also assumed this is why Liza had not contacted me as she said that she would.

With Liza now living in LaGrange, she was around more, visiting Paula and becoming more friendly to me. Liza's cousin has spoken with my husband and is at that time maintaining our lawn. My business is still in the red, but with steady growth, I project I will see green. Paula and I are still operating under our agreement, but there is a lot of stress on our business relationship. However, by this time, we had agreed with the owner of the property to lease purchase the facility we were renting and had rented out space to Liza's mother to operate a church. I believe it was because of such high stakes that Paula and my self continued to move forward with our arrangement, although there were distinct challenges in our business arrangement. My family and I started attending church services at Liza's mother's church. My husband Stephen was a deacon and his son, a junior deacon. I felt that I should support Liza's mother as she was renting space from Paula and me, and of course, my family wanted to help me. I became a student in the ministry studying under the guidance of liza's mother and became an ordained minister under her leadership.

I noticed that Liza was not her usual cheerful self. I speculated that she was sad because she had lost her job, and her son had caused her grief. "I need my church family to pray for me to find a job," said Liza, and we did pray for her. Several weeks later, Liza arrived at the church very happy. "I have a praise report," she stated. "I have just been offered a position working with the Governor's office, and the job pays $50,000 annually," she said. The entire congregation of about 7 people shouted for joy as she had been depressed and moody for weeks.

Liza and Paula seemed to have become very close and had closed-door meetings that did not involve me, or at least I was never invited to the meetings. Paula and I were continuing to have irreconcilable differences. The building was leaking. The renters were not able to pay their rent on time, along with other challenges. As a result, Liza's mother locates another building for her church and moves. Paula and I dissolved our business arrangement. I let the property go and found another location to rent. I continued operating my business at a new site. My family and I continue to attend church at Liza mother's new church location until it closes its doors again.

The year is now 2010, and Liza arrives at my new office location one day and indicates she believes I am positioned to perform work for the program she directs. She worked for a significant organization. I was not familiar with the program she spoke of, but I liked the sound of doing work for the organization. As a Certified Disadvantaged Business, I had been seeking contracts with a major organization for a long time. She asks, "would you be interested in developing some specialized training for a program that I am directing?"

I can't believe it, I think to myself. Being provided this opportunity is undoubtedly destiny. I ask her, "what type of training are you interested in?"

"Come by my office on Monday, and we will discuss it," she said.

I looked forward to meeting Liza on the following Monday. Liza's office was nestled in a professional building in downtown LaGrange. Her office location made sense since Liza indicated that a nationally recognized organization managed the program she administered. I arrive and take the elevator up to the second floor and walk into the office where Liza works. After introducing myself to the receptionist, Liza comes out to greet me. We move to her cubicle office area. We talk details regarding the training my office was to develop and deliver. She provides me with a verbal needs assessment regarding her staff as I took notes. Leaning into me, and speaking very low, she explained that her team was challenged as it relates to communicating in writing, and added, that often the reports that her staff submits were not satisfactory to management. She shared that when the reports are not acceptable, her program is not compensated. I listened very carefully; then, I shared with her some ideas for the specialized training that my company would develop and deliver for her team. She agreed, and asked me to "put together an outline of the training and a proposal." She also stated that her program is supervised by Leah, the Director of the organization.

Liza shares with me that while part of her job is to reach out to small disadvantaged businesses, she has to keep a lot of what she does under the radar to assist small black businesses. She said that the good old boy's network doesn't want black companies to have an opportunity. I nodded my head, indicating that I hear her. I had been trying for a very long time to do business with a significant organization and had no intention of allowing negativity to cripple my opportunity. Obtaining my certification as a Disadvantaged Business has in the past seemed to go unnoticed, until now. In my research, I understood that the Federal Government mandated that organizations receiving federal funds for their projects and programs were required to utilize the services of small businesses. Therefore, the work process that Liza discussed with me made sense at the time. The instinctive part of my mind rushed to affirm that which I had been believing and working toward.

(I now understand that one must evaluate everything. Especially when the thing appears to look like what you have believed for.)

I ask, "how are you going to keep the services provided to this program under the radar?"

"This is my program, my show, and I am the only one who has been trained in HIPPO. The Governor placed me over this program, and the Governor wants my office to utilize the services of small black businesses. I am not going to let the good old boy system have all the opportunities," said Liza. I thought to myself; finally, someone has been sent to assist small businesses. After that meeting, I regarded Liza with the highest esteem. My mind projected an image to myself that she cared about black-owned companies being given an opportunity.

(I think to myself; meeting Liza is like a dream come true. Finally, my hard work is paying off, and my company will be conducting business with the State of Georgia.)

My team and I developed the training and within several weeks the classes were commencing and being delivered in Liza's office as well as in my office. At various intervals, these classes were delivered in phases, coupled with out of class assignments, etc. The director of the organization sat in on one of the classes and seemed to enjoy it, and said as much. Observing the director's reaction to the class, I think to myself. She does not seem to have a problem with me as a small black business providing services. Perhaps Liza is mistaken, or maybe the director, who is a white female, is not part of the good old white boy network. At the same time, I also was aware that the good old boy system could shake your hand, pat you on your back, compliment you by saying 'good job,' while disliking you, and with plans in the back of their mind to terminate your services.

My company received positive reviews in a local newspaper article. This article was submitted to the news media by Liza's office upon my company, completing the first series of training. Again, I think she misspoke about her director not wanting to assist black small businesses as the newspaper article shouted the organization's support for my company and the specialized training we delivered. The huge article was positioned on the front page of the local newspaper. I felt such a sense of joy!

Liza was very supportive of my company, I thought. She connected my office with a program through another State organization to get trainees to assist the clerical needs of my office. In return, my office provided clerical and administrative skills training and seek full-time employment for the participants. These trainees were mothers with children who also required services from Liza's office. My company was compensated by Liza's program to train the participants and to provide a roster of available individuals to Liza for her program. I saw this as a "Win, Win." In the months and years to come, my office conducted a lot of business with the organization that Liza worked for. My office established separate business entities for cost accounting purposes and had my websites revamped to communicate more effectively to other like organizations across Georgia regarding the services my company offered. Liza informed me that she was part of a steering committee for the organization that positioned small businesses to participate in government contracts. She indicated that part of her responsibilities was to advise small businesses, such as mine, how to organize to attract more work with major organizations that are federally funded. It was my understanding that part of her job was to ensure small businesses were assisted to become part of a level playing field as it relates to programs administered by the organization she worked. Liza was also part of the Executive Board for a non-profit that I developed. She provided expertise on positioning strategy for the non-profit. It was Liza who also decided what work should be performed by the non-profit through her program. Positioning small businesses to participate in the contractual process all made sense to me. As a certified disadvantaged company, I was aware that large companies practiced this process.

Liza conducted several business forums from her home in LaGrange. At one of these business forums, I was introduced to business leaders who worked for the state, as well as other community small businesses. However, it was a unique introduction that Liza made only to me that I thought had placed my company in a prominent position. I was introduced to a person identified as the District Coordinator for her organization. Liza told me that she was only making this introduction to me because of my company's ability to develop and deliver specialized training and because I operated a business incubator. A business incubator is one that allows other businesses to rent space under their roof while providing training and other resources to assist the companies in becoming successful. In my mind, I thought this is amazing, now my office is not only doing business with a significant organization, but we are also in direct communication with the District Coordinator of that organization. Being in recognized in this light was undoubtedly a dream come true for my company.

(Research everyone and everything. Take nothing at face value when it comes to business)

The year was now 2011, and I had been conducting business with the organization through Liza for over a year. Business seemed good, but I had so many personal challenges, I lost a brother to cancer and a sister to heart disease, and then, my late husband Stephen was unexpectedly killed in a trucking accident. I found a way to move past the hurt, and was remarried in 2013 and relocated to Alabama. After getting settled, I called Leah, the director of the organization, as I wanted to make sure she was satisfied with my past services and to ask if there were any future work. I had been out of the loop since the untimely death of my loved ones, and since my services were requested on an as-needed basis, I wanted to make sure my company's past consultant services had not been forgotten. The director answers, we chat, and I ask if the organization is satisfied with my company's past services. "I don't have any complaints regarding your services, but you must speak with Liza as she handles those matters," said Leah. I wanted to ask about some other concerns that I had, but she seemed rushed, and as I started forming another question, she stated again, "contact Liza with any questions you have." I thanked her, and we ended the call.

I did contact Liza the next day. However, she was already aware that I had contacted her office and spoken with Leah. After the initial greeting and pleasantries, she said, "you are aware that I am the person responsible for selecting the companies who perform services for my program, aren't you?" Before I could respond, she said, "I thought you understood that." She continued, "you contacted Leah yesterday, causing it to appear that I am not assisting small businesses."

"I asked for you, but your assistant told me you were not available," I said to her.

"You may want to remember what I told you about the good old boys," said Liza. I apologized for overreaching; she didn't comment on my apology. She began discussing some upcoming business opportunities with me.

My business continued to provide services to the program directed by Liza through the organization. Although in my thoughts, I questioned the organization's work processes from incorrect addresses on my checks, misuse of my company's name on the checks sent to me, not receiving 1099 for tax purposes, the method in which they managed verbal requisitions for services, and my company having to be responsible for receiving all payments for any work performed, I continued providing services for the organization. I worked on even as I was held accountable for coordinating performances that I could not validate. I was told by Liza that I am performing work under a HIPPO grant, and the grant dictates to the organization, the work process that must be adhered to.

"All work must flow through the small business," said Liza. Liza's spoken words seemed to be true since she was continually pushing me to deposit my earned checks so that the District Coordinator could receive the funds to pay the counselors they had secured through my research.

(I now understand when intuition speaks, listen. Our intuition speaks softly. It is not demanding and one must pay attention to hear).

While it appeared to me that Liza, through the organization, utilized unconventional business practices, it seemed that her organization was on board with her method of operation. I was invited and attended events sponsored by Liza's office, and even her wedding.

These events were also accompanied by Leah, who is the organization's Director, other organizational office personnel, and even the organization's Board Members. At some of the events, I was given the opportunity to speak of my ongoing work with the organization and was always greeted with a smile, a pat on the back, and with a keep up the good work comment from management.

(I had no idea that behind the smiles, a storm was brewing, and I was directly in its path).

(Understanding my personal-self caused me to recognize that I have always operated from established rules. When I reflect on the things that have built my values in life, I realized they were rules that seemed to keep me safe from the horrors of growing up in a white-dominated society such as North Carolina in the sixties. I have always been a "by the book" individual. Personality assessments that I have taken documented this trait. Although, I had grown and, in my mind, have shed some of the ideas that rules are established for my good. I never have been able to abandon the total concept of not staying within established rules, especially those handed down from those who seem to have authority)

As a service provider who trusted those placed in leadership positions, I performed services in accordance with the instructions provided. Also, having already been chastised by Liza… I decided that if I wanted to continue my work with the organization; I needed to trust her to do her job; after all, Liza is in a public trust position, speaking of public trust let's look at…

Chapter 9

Meanwhile
Back In Captivity
Shifting Pain Into Power

Officer, I need some toilet paper! I am on my monthly, the one roll I got last week is gone, plus I shared the role I had with other people, screamed the captive! Sounds like a personal problem, "you give yours away, then you go without," said the officer. Now, you are going to have to wait until we get some more tissue, shrieked the officer from the perch in the locked bubble that served as the watchtower looking down into the dorm that held the captives. I need some tissue too, said another captive. I thought to myself, I only have little tissue left, I hope the tissue comes in soon enough, and for the first time in my life, I was concerned about getting toilet paper so I could use the bathroom.

(*I am now alerted to the fact that the system that captured individuals were not providing for their basic needs in a timely manner.* I observed that the prison system punishes a captive for sharing and promotes an atmosphere of self-survival.)

Captives who have family support on the outside to put money on their books could afford to buy food, clothes, and humanitarian items, such as toilet paper. Those captives who had no outside support either became sex slaves of those who have worked for those who have or stole from those who have. And any of those reasons most often caused an argument which leads to fighting among the captives. Through the guidance of my ancient ancestors, I realized that although I was being held a captive in the system, I mentally choose not to become a victim. Instead, my ancestors urged me to observe and analyze the penal system in which I had been captured. I would help other captives to become woke so that they could see the real enemy, even as they screamed on the inside.

Taking my eyes off the external world and placing them on the internal, "I" saved my life. Sitting quietly, thinking, I remembered the truth that had been hidden within me for a time, such as the darkening days. From a place within that I had never ventured, I remembered that power and fearlessness are my divine heritage. From that moment, I started walking and exercising daily. Space was limited in Troup County Jail, but I knew that I needed to do this. One day as I begin my daily exercise routine, other captives say, hold up Ms. Ann, we want to work out with you. Other captives are walking and exercising with me, and asking me for advice. Officers did not like this and would often demand that we sit on our bunks for hours at a time, and this, of course, would cause the arguments to flame again. I was told by a captive that being restrained to the bunks provided too much time for her to think. She told me that she often thought of her children that she left in someone else's care; be reminded of the fate that was waiting for them just around the corner, their desires, and needs, and when all these thoughts took over, then anger would burst through like a burglar kicking in a locked door, she explained this with tears in her eyes. As a result, I understood that a single comment could spark an already internally inflamed captive. I began to observe that most of the disagreements occurred on the weekend. I determined it was because captives had endured verbal abuse from the officers all week, and on the weekend, were bored and most often hungry. Captives did not receive lunch on the weekends, and if they did not have money to purchase from the online store, the early dinner that they were served left them hungry in the evening. The cycle of oppression for captives was never-ending. Some of those who opened up to me about their past had been raped as a child, had mental challenges, were from broken homes, and had already been in the system more times than they could count. Charges seem to start with writing a bad check to purchase food for their children, after which, the smaller crimes would escalate. For most, they had been on probation, and could not pay the fees and fines, and were hiding out until they were caught, now the individual was faced with more time in jail or are being sent away to prison. The captured individual spoke of wanting something more, but the lack of education or just having confidence seemed to always place their desires out of reach. **Once a captured individual said to me, "I wish I had never been born."**

(Yes, there is a cycle of oppression for some of those being captured and held in captivity.)

Officers screamed and cursed at captives when they asked for anything throughout the week. They ignored their cry for assistance on the weekend, and they had their way with captives who were hungry. I was awakened in the early morning hours and witnessed an officer taking a captive out of the dorm. I wondered if anyone else was seeing what I was witnessing. I overheard that captive later telling others that she was having sex with the officer.

The other captives laughed at her, saying, "girl, you lay down with anybody for an extra sandwich."

The violated female did not seem to display any shame. Instead, she said, "An extra sandwich, you better make that an extra tray bit--." I understand that this officer was later terminated.

The tolerated sexual abuse, the arguments, and fights demonstrated to me that the captives were stressed and believed they had no other recourse. Captives used their bodies for what they thought they needed and took their frustrations out on each other through fighting. I decided to think of solutions that would serve for a more harmonious atmosphere for my personal-self versus identifying with the injustice being served by the officials. I asked one of the seemly conscious officers if we, the captives, could have a talent show. "I don't care, as long as you don't disturb me," said the frowned face officer. Eagerly, I began making plans for the talent show.

I announced the upcoming talent show to the captives regarding the talent show, and what the prize to the winner would be. The winner would be given food items from the prison store along with toilet paper that was also available on the store. I used part of the money that my family sent to me for my upkeep to purchase these items. I didn't have a lot of money, but some of the other captives had nothing. Those captives who had more had already been trained by the system to be self-absorbent. In other words, in their minds, they had only enough for themselves, and they were attached to the material possessions, and would not share. I decided that I would not allow the system to train me to have a self-absorbent mindset. I had seen enough of the organized justice system to realize that the system is designed to separate and conquer. It is designed to break your will and cause an individual to depend on the system; therefore, following the system's rules, I moved in the positive vibration of what I believed a judicial, correctional system should be. I got busy working on the talent show that I believed would rehabilitate captives. If only for a moment they would be working together. I choose and appointed judges and developed criteria that the participants would be judged by. The captives were very excited. They used whatever material they could find for designing costumes for themselves, they huddled together for practice, working as teams to present their best in the talent show. The event was scheduled to be held on a Friday, and the participants had an entire week to become prepared. It was so much fun to watch the captives work together, even as a single captive tried to cause a problem during the event, the other captives voted her out of the dorm. She was removed by an officer on duty immediately. The event was very successful! The Joker, Tiny, and Lus hugged me and said, "Ms. Ann, we will never forget you." Neither of them seemed to care that the Joker had won the talent show and got the prize, I noticed the Joker sharing the award with others. There were no fights that weekend as everyone seemed to be on a natural high regarding the show. You could hear conversations throughout the dorm talking about how much fun they had, and even talking about the next show.

A week after the talent show, I was awakened, "pack it up Spell, pack it up," said the screaming voice of the officer located in the tower hovering over the Pod.

My heart leaped like a deer fleeing from hunters during deer season. I realized this day was coming, but I had hoped this cup was passed from me, and I would be released from jail to return to my family. Silently, my inner being communicates with my mind. (**"You are fearless."**) I had to believe this because now I was being transported to prison. Not only had I never been in jail before, but I had also never been in prison. I was not even allowed to contact my family to let them know what was happening to me, nor did I know where I was being taken.

It seemed that everyone in the dorm wanted to hug me goodbye, and they were, but they were also there to take possession of anything that I could not take with me. Food and any other item they could seize; you see, the system is set up, so a captive is required to throw away all things that they purchased in the county jail, therefore when the captive arrives at the prison camp, they must repurchase all the items again. This is everything except for envelopes, stamps, and a bible. And, you can only have one bible.

Again, I am chained; but this time, I am placed in the back seat of a regular vehicle. I think, at least it's not a dog transport vehicle. I am alone for the more than two and half-hour ride while being handcuffed, chained, and feet shackled together. My physical body does not understand why my mind has not given it the order to cry out in panic.

(On the outside of me, I felt like a destroyer was moving soundlessly in my world, but at that very moment, I decided and willed my mind to choose what I would feel. I sat back, watched the trees and grass along the side of the roadway wave and bow to me as the vehicle transporting me drove forward, without my approval, leaving behind my family, my friends, my business and my past. My thoughts sneak back and reflect again on the path that leads me here.)

Chapter 10

Reflecting
The Whisper of Fate
The Raging Storm Arrives
Sacrifice Led to Slaughter

Life seems to be going well. My husband and I were approved to purchase a new home and were preparing to move into it. One day as I was moving about outside of our current home in Talladega, Alabama, I felt a jolt of fear rushed to my chest. It felt like a gust of strong wind landed a punch within me. And then, a thought illuminated within my mind.

"When you move into your new home, trouble will come."

As suddenly as the idea came, it seemed to blow away as fast. A gust of wind seemed to capture it, and the thought vanished, but not before my mind reflected on Liza. My immediate thought is that something may have happened to her. I pull out my cell phone and call her. "Hey, is everything ok?" I ask.

"Yes," she stated. I did not tell her of the thought that had paraded on my mental stage. I was checking on you, I told her. She provided some details about another assignment, and we ended the call.

Several weeks after my husband and I moved into our new home, I received a call at my office in Lincoln, Alabama, from Liza. "I have been terminated," she said to me.

I am flabbergasted. I asked, "why are you being terminated?"

"Embezzlement," she said.

"Why are they doing this to you?" I ask.

"I told you they would not like black businesses having an opportunity. It's the good old boys; they are saying that the counselors have not been providing counseling for the children," she said.

I laugh, "all you have to do is to have the counselors come forward. They know that your office was compensating them, and you know that they provided the services," I say to her.

"The counselors are not going to want to do that because they are moonlighting and are being paid on 1099," she said. She interrupted me as I started to speak, I will call you back, she said.

After several days, I wondered why Liza had not contacted me again. I reflected over time and realized that Liza had not sent me any 1099s for the work I performed and was paid for even though I had been asking for them. I wanted to believe that it was just sloppy bookkeeping on the part of the organization. At this point, I am also hoping that Liza will get me the proper documents. Then I remember that she was terminated.

(A weight of despair started to form in my chest and the intuition vibrations that I had ignored in the past. I was now listening to them, and they were screaming within me. Talk to Liza, find out what is going on, something is not right, a scream within said.)

I call Liza to understand what is happening. She told me that officials are investigating everyone that conducted business with my Program. "They are probably going to come to see you because you conducted business with my office, but you have no reason to worry. You didn't do anything wrong," she stated.

I knew I had not done anything wrong; I was concerned about Liza and the documents that I was still waiting for her to provide me so that I could adequately file my taxes. I believed as she had alleged that she was being set up. I reminded Liza again that her office had not yet forwarded me appropriate documents for filing my taxes. I am now concerned that management may use this against me. I said this to Liza.

"Liza, you must bring all the people forward who performed work on this project. Bring in the counselors and the District Coordinator," I said.

"I have been trying to contact the District Coordinator, but she has not responded," she said. I sensed the anger in her response. "If I go down Leah is going down with me. She knows what's going on. It was Leah's responsibility to ensure that the work that the counselors were assigned to do was being performed. She is the director, not me. She is doing this because I choose to use black consultants, and she wanted only her white friends to get all of the work," stated Liza. "I will not let her get away with this," she said.

I am listening, not wanting to believe what I am hearing. I did not want to consider what was being alleged by Liza, that the director of the Organization was destroying Liza because Liza had chosen to utilize consultants of color. "Why would she do this to you? Leah knew that my company was performing services. She sat in during a class session," I said. "Did you also use counselors of color, is this why Leah is upset," I asked?

Raising her voice, "she is trying to cast blames on me, and she will not get away with it," Liza said again.

I ask again, "where is the District Coordinator?"

"I have not seen her since I was terminated," Liza said.

"You haven't heard from her! You told me she was the person who paid the counselors, and I still do not have 1099s for those expenses," I explain to Liza. "Perhaps she is traveling out of town," I say.

"Don't worry, I am not going to put you in something you didn't do," Liza remarked. "I know," I say in response.

"If investigators come to see me, I will tell the truth," I tell her. "We need to meet, but you live in Alabama, and authorities told me that I could not leave the State," Liza said.

"Ok," I say, but Liza and I never meet. When I got home, I told my family what has happened to Liza; we did not worry as I related to them that I believed after the investigators complete their work, it would prove that Liza had done nothing wrong. I was never concerned about myself as I knew that I had not committed any offenses, and I believed as Liza had led me to think that Leah was out to get her.

(I had no idea I was a lamb being led to slaughter by the very person I trusted and respected.)

I did not hear from Liza for a couple of weeks. I keep calling her because I had previously paid her to perform a show she played a character, one that was very popular locally. I needed to make sure she was still going to deliver as she had already been paid. And those responsible for supporting the event needed to be told or least be refunded their money. I assumed she would cancel because the event was to be held in Alabama, and she had said to me that she could not leave the State of Georgia.

A week or two later, my staff and I are working in my office located in Lincoln, Alabama. Two men walk in; my assistant greets them. They were investigators from the City of LaGrange. My assistant leads them to my office. I could sense fear waking up and beating a drum on my heart that caused it to race ahead of my thoughts. Where is this feeling coming from, I think to myself? I have done nothing wrong, thinking to myself.

As I recount the events of that day and reflect inwardly.

(I now realize that I had been mentally trained to fear and obey those in authority. Fear is the emotion that somehow in my past, I had associated with those in authority, even as I knew I had done nothing wrong and believed I had no reason to fear. Now I understand the fear that I sensed existed as a result of growing up in the age of segregation. I witnessed dogs being

used against students by those in authority as we sat on a school bus. We were not allowed to get off the bus. Those who wore faces of hate screamed threats of violence at the students of color whose only crime was wanting to attend school. The fear that I thought had disappeared long ago remained within. This deep-rooted fear leaves an imprint on your psyche. It hides and only screams from the inside.)

    The investigators walk into my office, and I offer them a seat. They give me some background regarding the purpose of their visit. They ask if I mind speaking with them, I say not a problem. Me even speaking with the investigators was a grave error in judgment on my part. Speaking with investigators without being represented by an attorney is not something anyone should ever do. I was told by the investigator that I was not a suspect. They said they just wanted to get the facts, and then asked if I mind signing a document agreeing to speak with them. My intellectual mind urged me not to talk with them without an attorney being present, but my instinctive mind answered with the force of fear and whispered to my human self. If you don't speak with these authority figures, they are going to think you did something wrong. I allowed the fear of those in authority to lead me on an untraveled path. The investigators said, before completing what I know now to be an interrogation. "Liza has implicated you and Leah as the persons that have committed a crime."

    "I can't believe Liza would tell such a lie," I say to them.

    "She wants you and Leah to take the fall for this," they say. I think to myself; they are part of the good old boy network. They are trying to hurt Liza because she supports black businesses. I had witnessed this system operate within the business industry on many occasions.

After a brief pause, I say, "I have told you the facts as I know them. If Liza tells the truth, and I believe she will, you will get this sorted out."

As the investigators stand to leave, they turn and say. "Think about what we said. We will be in touch if we need further clarification."

I call Liza to relay to her what the investigators said. She said, "They are trying to scare you. You did nothing wrong," she said.

Liza continues to fill me in on what she wanted me to know, and I now realize that she needed to know what I had said to the investigators. Liza continues, "the authorities came to my home and took my phone and computer. I had to get another phone. "I have not contacted you for this reason," she explained.

"Did you tell them the truth about me performing services for your organization?" I ask. "The investigators told me that you are trying to set Leah and me up," I say to her.

"They are trying to turn you against me because they are upset that I am telling on Leah, don't believe them. Anyway, you provided a service and was paid for it; there is no law against that," stated Liza.

"I told them the truth as I know it," I said. I then ask Liza, "Is there anything that I should be concerned about?"

She told me, "No, you did nothing wrong; they are trying to cover for Leah."

Several weeks later, investigators from the City of LaGrange and Talladega County arrive at my office as my staff, and I sat working. "We are still trying to piece everything together," the lead investigator said, "and I believe you and Leah are victims of Liza," he stated. "We need to review your files to pull the final report together," the investigator tells me.

The investigation is finally coming to an end, I think to myself. "What makes you think that Liza did this?" I ask.

"She misled Leah as she did you," responded the investigator. "She made Leah believe that because she was the person trained in the HIPPO Law, certain information was off-limits to those who had not attended the training," stated the lead investigator. However, in my mind, I still believed that Leah was trying to set Liza up. I allowed the investigators to review my files. Again, another error in judgment.

The investigators explain that they need to get data for clarification. "Do you mind signing a document agreeing to allow us to look around," asked the lead investigator?

Thinking to myself, I have nothing to hide, so I say, no problem. Investigators review and take some files and ledgers, but the information as far as I could ascertain had nothing to do with my work with the organization. I was not authorized to maintain data because of the HIPPO Law or the services performed because of the law, according to and as directed by Liza. The lead investigator from the City of LaGrange asked if I would provide my bank records. I say no problem. He leaves me his business card as a source of contact. Within two weeks, I obtain my bank records and call the investigator to let him know I have them. The investigator never returns my repeated phone calls. I assume they have what they needed, and the investigation is over.

During the almost two years that followed, I spoke to Liza periodically. She continued to say that she has evidence to prove that Leah was the person trying to set her up. She seemed to be upset that the organization had not given her job back. She said that the local newspaper indicated that she and I were not suspects. I was not privileged to the local news of LaGrange, and since no one had contacted me again, I thought this nightmare was over for me.

(*I think to myself, perhaps the investigators discovered that Liza and I were innocent. Maybe they now know that Leah is guilty, and because they have found that Leah did this, they are going to sweep it under the rug. I say to myself. It always happens like this.*)

I did not understand, however, why Liza was not reinstated to her position. No wonder she is upset, I say to myself. Liza shared that the investigators were still looking for answers, but that we were not included in that investigation. She said that she had made it clear that I provided services for the money I was paid. She had also secured an attorney. I had not obtained one as I believed that my circumstances did not warrant legal representation. I continued to trust Liza. She had not given me cause not to believe her, although something within me kept nudging me to wake up.

CHAPTER 11

Reflecting
The Trap Was Set
The Initial Capture was Formality

I remember my granny saying, baby, hindsight is twenty-twenty. I never thought about what she meant by that statement until two Talladega officers were handcuffing me. The officers advised me that I was being placed under arrest. It was on a Friday morning. One staff member was in the office with me. Everyone else was off for the day. I sent that staff member home, closed my office and called my husband to let him know that I was being arrested, but there was nothing he could do. The officers could not tell me why I was being detained. They only stated that I was being held because I fled a crime in another State. The City of LaGrange had sworn out a warrant for my arrest, saying that I escaped the State after committing a crime by seeking residence in another State. I was shocked to learn this as I had been cooperating with investigators since being contacted and had even left messages for the lead investigator that I had my bank records available for his review. My arrest was based on a lie and underlined with injustice even from the very beginning.

Because it was a Friday, Troup County would not come to pick me up until that coming Monday. Therefore, I was caged in Talladega County Jail for the entire weekend. I could not be offered or post bail until I was transported from Talladega to Troup County. It was not until I was taken before the judge in Talladega County on Monday morning that my rights were read to me. I thought this was strange. I was advised that this is the new way that a captured person's rights are read to them. It seems the system was losing too many cases by not following the law of reading of the rights before arrest; therefore, the system wrote a new law to get around it. Capture an individual, put them in a cage, which does not allow the captured individual to search and interview and secure an attorney. Then read the captured individual their rights, advising the captured individual of their right to obtain an attorney.

(I discovered that having a right does not grant you access; your access is limited because you are locked in a cage. Besides, the money that could have been used to obtain an attorney must now be used to bond out of jail. A person is indicted in Georgia by the Grand Jury. The Grand Jury does not invite the one being charged, nor does your attorney need to attend.

(The judicial process was never intended to serve justice. It was and is, a process to capture "Just Us.")

That weekend seemed like the worst of my entire life. I had never been in jail as a captive. I had only toured them. The Talladega jail was not fit for human habitation. When an individual would use the restroom, men and others walking by could view their nakedness. It was shameful. I endured the weekend, and after attending the arraignment on Monday morning, where my rights were finally read, I was then transported to Troup County jail on Sam Walker Drive in LaGrange.

In Troup County, the conditions were worse than Talladega as the jail held more captives. I was not given a bunk, mat, blanket, clothes, and was not allowed to take a shower. Finally, on a Wednesday afternoon, an officer opened the cage and called for me. I thought I was going to be given a phone call and allowed to take a bath. This was not the case; a City of LaGrange officer appeared after I was taken out of the holding cage. "You do want to talk to the investigator," he said.

"I guess," I replied.

(My thoughts were, perhaps they made a mistake in arresting me, and now they have sorted things out. *Another error in my judgment).*

The officer handcuffed me, led me outside, and placed me in the back of a police squad car. I still had not had a bath, had not been given toiletries in order to brush my teeth, and had not even been given a washcloth to wash my face. I was emotionally stressed and should not have been speaking with any investigator. Especially to one whose only intention was to have me indicted for something I was not guilty of committing. However, at that time, I wanted everyone to know that I have nothing to hide; therefore, I continue to allow myself to be led to the slaughter. At the time, I had not realized that the system had already made up its mind about me and now needed me to participate in the plan and assist them in carrying out their plan of injustice. Unknowingly, I helped the system to enslave my physical self by trying to defend myself in a legal system that is woven in injustice. The same prejudice that was deeply rooted in a system's desire to purchase, capture, and enslave my ancestors.

(**Make no mistake about it. The slave entitlement attitude was passed down by the ancestors of those who seek even through their offspring to continue enslavement. This is a learned system being demonstrated in the offspring of those long past. This evidence is apparent in the wording of Amendment XIII of the US Constitution. Why else are persons sentenced to prison being defined as a slave? They are called our forefathers; I call them the "Willie Lynch System."**)

(*Don't take my word for it, read the constitution for yourself.*) *Think about this; did you see any person resembling persons of color assisting in the implementation of the constitution of the United States, or was it written by those who shoved it down our throats.*)

I was taken to the City of LaGrange police department, removed from the car and transported to a hallway. I was then handcuffed and chained to a chair. The same investigator who came to see me in my office in Lincoln, Alabama, went into the small hallway, introduces himself as if I didn't remember him. "I want to ask you a few questions," he said. "We are trying to get to the bottom of this. I believe you and Leah are victims," he said while looking directly in my eyes. I looked at the investigator, trying to gauge if he is honest.

"Why did the City of LaGrange lie in the warrant for my arrest? I cooperated and even tried to reach you to provide the bank records you requested," I said to him.

"That was how the warrant had to be worded, just a technicality," said the investigator.

I wanted to believe him. I wanted this to be over, I desired to go back to my normal life where I operated a business, attended church, and spent quality time with my family. I didn't realize that everything that my family and I had known was about to be changed forever.

While chained to a chair, I answered questions. I said the same truths as I had stated when the investigators came to my office in Alabama. I was finally taken back to the jail and placed back in a cage with other captives. The next day I was retaken from the cage, brought back to the City of LaGrange police department. Again, I was chained to a chair and handcuffed; however, this time, the interrogation was conducted by a person identified as a financial expert. Also in attendance was a female who worked for the expert and the City of LaGrange investigator.

At the end of the interrogation, I was told by the investigator that "I am going to speak with the DA on your behalf," but now, I was not trusting anyone, the investigator, nor Liza, or those who represented the system. I had not spoken to my family, but I realized that these people were not out for justice. I asked several times to use the phone but was not allowed. There was a phone located inside the holding cell, but I did not have a PIN code to activate it. Even if I wanted an attorney to come and see me, I could not have contacted one or even my family.

I was finally able to go before a judge on an electronic screen who was able to set a bond. My daughter arrived back from a trip to Jamaica to assist my husband in posting my bond as he told my family that he did not have the money to post my bond. I discovered that my bond had been posted while I was still being interrogated. Even after my bond was posted, the investigator tried to hold me and ask more questions. I yet had not had a bath or brushed my teeth. I had on the same clothes I had been arrested in. I told the investigator that I was tired and wanted to go to my family. The investigator had no choice but to allow me to be taken back to the jail so I could be released on bond to my family.

I was so embarrassed as I was released and walked out to my family, who was waiting for me. I was embarrassed because I smell, and I knew it. I was embarrassed because my family, who has always looked up to me, now, had to bond me out of jail. As I reflected back on that moment, I sensed a pocket of sadness growing from a root within me that long ago had given place to this emotion.

"Hello, Mom," my family smiles and says, "We got you." They pull me close and hug me tight even though my body smells foul. I felt safe. Every member of my family living in Georgia travel back with me to Alabama, where I had lived for the past four and a half years. I now realize that I need to hire an attorney, but I am a small business, and getting money for an attorney is not going to be easy. I now realize that I should have never spoken to investigators without the presence of an attorney, even as I knew I am innocent.

My daughter and I started looking for legal representation. I am also going into my office trying to keep my business up and operating to earn money to pay a lawyer.

(I repeat the words of a well-known scripture; "no weapon formed against me shall prosper." Still, my feelings gave me a different report, and my thoughts guided by my mind was like a high-speed passenger train, stopping and going, picking up passengers at every stop; passengers that vibrated both negative and positive energy.)

Liza called me, "I was arrested and bonded out," she said.

"Liza, I don't understand. If you told the investigators the truth, why did they arrest me?" I ask her.

"They are trying to scare you so they can save Leah," she said.

Finally, I listened to her and perceived the truth that until now, I had been unwilling to believe. I thought to myself, that statement does not make any sense. Then as I reflected, Liza's past comments seemed to float before my mind's eye. As a darken sky suddenly illuminated with light, my mind held the truth before me. I could now clearly see that the directives Liza had given me, the work processes she directed and utilized, did not make business sense. In my heart, I thought she was concerned with ensuring small black businesses were afforded an opportunity on the playing field. After all, this is what I had always believed in and advocated. However, I realized that my personality desired the feeling of the success of having performed work for a major organization to be listed on my resume to such a degree that I was able to be blindsided. My personality tolerated and feed my emotional state of being regarding system injustices; therefore, it was easy to accept and believe Liza. Liza and I had spoken on many issues of injustice that moved me. She used my desire for disadvantaged businesses to be given a level playing field to manipulate me. My state of emotions guided my thoughts, led my mind to perceive, and believe that Liza, who was in a position of authority, had my best interest at heart. Another error in judgment.

*(**The mistake was to underestimate the intention of people who hold positions of authority because they look like me. It was at this point that I tuned in and listened to my intuition. I realized that it was every individual for themselves**).*

Liza asked me to meet with her and her attorney. She said, "you are probably going to be upset with me, but we need to meet with my attorney together." However, I no longer trusted Liza, and had decided to obtain my attorney. I did not tell her this as I had decided to limit my conversations with her.

On the day that I was due to meet with Liza and her attorney, I had retained an attorney. Liza sent me a text asking if I was going to join the meeting. I responded, "I can't." I then choose not to communicate with her anymore.

After borrowing money from my husband for a retainer, I secured the attorney. Yes, borrow! I had to pay his money back to him! I provided the attorney with my tax documents, bank statements, list of witnesses, text and email messages, Secretary of State documents, EIN numbers, and other related documents that would demonstrate my business operations. I also provided texted correspondence from Liza that she had sent me. My testimony had not changed. I provided the State with the same truth earlier. The same information was provided to my trial attorney 30 to 45 days after he was hired. My attorney advised, as I already had decided, not to communicate with Liza any longer.

At this point in time, the attorney had been hired for at least a year and had not done anything that he informed me of. My daughter that assisted me in locating the attorney advised that I call him to get a status update, and I did call him. The attorney answered and said he was going to set up a date for us to meet. After some months had swirled by, the attorney called me. We met and discussed options regarding the case. "The State is offering you a plea," he said. "Wouldn't a plea mean that I am guilty and did something wrong," I ask. "Yes," he said. "We can take the fight to them and prove your innocence, but it is my job to let you know of the plea," he said. "The City of LaGrange is a racist city, but we will prove that it was Liza who did this and not you," he said. I agreed to the fight. After all, I had already told them the truth, and obviously, the State had not accepted it. I believed the jury would see the truth. I asked my attorney why the State did not believe me.

"The State needs two people to prove a conspiracy," he said, "and you and Liza make up the two. They are not willing to look at Leah as she is white," he said.

My attorney and I would see Liza on the many over 2-hour trips back and forth to court. She would whisper to me as I would pass her. "I love you, sister." I even thought that she would come forward and tell the truth. I believed this until I was shown a video by my attorney of Liza making her plea on video. The plea where she lied about the nature of my involvement to receive a lesser sentence for herself.

I was continually offered the same plea of five years before Liza accepted the same plea. I could not see myself taking a plea for something that I did not do, nor could I see myself going to prison for a crime I did not commit. I had told the truth as I had known it and believed the truth would set me free. I believed justice would prevail. I pondered on my legal state of affairs often, but I did not give a lot of thought regarding the attorney that I had hired. I should have.! I trusted him to do what he was hired to do. I never thought about the fact that he never deposed the State prosecutor's prime witnesses. He went on a vacation a week prior to my trial and left his assistant, who played in a band on weekends to call my witnesses on the phone a week before trial. I should have given more consideration to the past articles I had read of the countless accounts of black women being sentenced to an enormous number of years in prison for nonviolent offenses in the State of Georgia as a result of an unjust legal system, and as a result of ineffective counsel. I never considered the fact that Liza had taken a plea, so how was my attorney going to place the blame where it should be.

(Trust only the higher power within)

I was nudged within my inner self to terminate the attorney during trial, as he may have objected to the State Prosecutors once, talked to the State prosecutors like they were his best friends while saying to me that the town was the racist party of the good old boys; but I refused to raise the issue of race during trial. He told me the jury would get upset if he used the race card. **My attorney's demonstration of practicing** *law, in my opinion, is why so many people are in prison for crimes they did not commit.*

There was an occasion where I had taken the elevator to go to lunch when the court had recessed. An individual who was alone with me in the elevator said, "you must have an excellent attorney if you are going to trial in LaGrange."

My mind misinterpreted the individual's point. I thought the individual was asking me a question regarding the expertise of my attorney. As usual, my untrained mind at that time, allowed my mouth to speak before the essence of the words the individual said to me were clear. "Do you want the contact information for my attorney," I ask?

"No," said the individual. "I'm just saying, I hope he is really good." The elevator door opens, and the individual walks off. I did not think any more about the remarks of the gentleman until I began this book.

(*The Universe's love for me continued to show me the light, but I didn't understand. You see Reader, I believed that the light would shine injustice, but now I am reminded of the scripture that indicates, "justice stands far off; for truth is fallen in the street, and equity cannot enter."*)

The fear of having no defense to represent me froze my physical ability to terminate my attorney, even as I was witnessing the ineffectiveness of his counsel. It wasn't like I had more money to hire someone else, and I was not sure of how long the State would allow me to find another attorney. Thinking I had no other options, I continue believing that through the God in heaven, the jury would see the truth, believing that the jury would understand that I would not do the things being stated about me by the District Attorney. What I did not realize is that the jury or judge was not going to hear my testimony? The investigator for the State decided in court to withhold the testimony that had been taken from me when they had me deliver it to them from the Troup County jail, and my attorney agreed with their decision in a subtle way. I remember my attorney saying, "the prosecution is not going to show your testimony." I look at him and ask, "how will they hear my side?"

My attorney states again, "we will show this was a scheme executed by Liza

My attorney said, "you have a right to take the stand, but I don't think we need you to take the stand. We can win without you taking the stand."

I asked him, "how will the jury and the judge hear my side."

"I am going to demonstrate to the State that you were a victim just like Leah," he stated to me. "We will use the testimony of Liza to prove your innocence," he said.

What my attorney did not care to think about, and my limited knowledge of the so-called justice system did not alert was that Liza had already played the game of, **"let's make a deal."**

She made this clear while testifying on behalf of the State. *"I know one thing, I can only serve five years in prison," she said while rolling her eyes at my attorney and me. She realized something my attorney should have known. She had already admitted guilt. She had been bought, sold, and saved by the State of Georgia.* What did she care about the truth at this point? She had only to pay her debt to the State. It did not matter that she had a prior felony for a similar offense in another State. She was still hired in a public trust position to oversee disbursements and administer contracts. It did not matter that the Organization did not bother to conduct a proper background check. It did not matter that she, in the past, had been reprimanded verbally as a result of using the organization's credit card for personal use for thousands of dollars and it did not matter that in her own testimony, Liza said that everyone in her organization's office with the exception of two people were stealing money from the funds donated to the organization. This testimony was not introduced in court by my attorney. When on break, I ask him why he was not presenting the evidence, *"we are winning," said my attorney.*

(Now, I understand that the "We" he referred to me was "them")

It was the night before the last day of the three-day trial. I received a call at approximately 9:00 PM. Hello Ms. Spell, my heart begins racing. I think to myself; something must be wrong for my attorney to be calling this time of the night. "I don't think we need to have your witnesses to appear tomorrow. I called a prosecutor friend of mine, and he said that if we are doing well without witnesses, it is best not to call them as they may open the door to scrutiny," stated my attorney.

I think to myself, tomorrow is the last day of my trial; but I say, "if you say so." I further stated, "you are the professional, and would know best. I still don't understand how the judge and jury will hear my side," I say.

"The burden is on the State to prove you guilty, and they have failed to prove that," he said. "Your testimony and the testimony of Leah are identical," he stated.

Intuition nudged me, remember the State refused to show your testimony, the judge and jury have not heard your statement, nudged my intuition.

(My lower instinctive mind reasoned and made the decision; this is why you hired legal counsel to represent you. Let legal counsel guide you, I reasoned with myself. (How did that work out for me? If you don't remember, go back and read the first chapter of this book).

(I step back for a moment to say something that I want every reader of this book to remember. I believe that Oprah Winfrey said to make sure that you sign your checks. Well, let me tell you this; never put your life in the hands of an attorney, paid or otherwise. I don't care how good you may think they are or have heard or read how successful they are. Act as an assistant to the hired attorney in your case; make sure that this information is a matter of record in the courts. There is no other person that can or will tell your truth as you can, and no one will fight for your cause like you. I don't care how much money you pay them; otherwise, you may become a captive of the prison slave camp.)

Chapter 12

Meanwhile
Destination
Prison Slave Camp at Diagnostics
The Encounter
No More Reflecting

I become aware that the vehicle transporting me to Lee Annandale State Prison is slowing down. My senses focus back to the present. The car comes to a complete stop in front of an old red brick building complex that appears it was constructed in the 1920s. I am taken from the car, my feet remain shackled, and my hands remain handcuffed. The officer signs documents to release me, their latest captive to the prison slave camp. The shackles and handcuffs are removed, and the receiving officer takes charge.

Stand against the wall in a straight line. The officer is screaming out commands to me and many other captives that have just arrived. The fear that arose within me now was fear of the unknown. These officers were majority white with skinned heads. There was no evidence of empathy or just simple humanity anywhere in the room. The room was dismal, and the walls seem to be painted with the color of sorrow. I was in a place where I had never been to before, and I had no idea what would happen. We were all told to undress so that we could be inspected. Every word spoken to us was seasoned with contempt and served with harshness. I can only imagine what my ancestors felt like when they were being examined before being sold to the highest bidder. I felt like a lump of meat that is being inspected by a butcher.

(Time seemed to slow down, or was my pulse beating more slowly? I could not be sure as everything seemed so intense, but moving slowly, and just like before, I sensed the presence of my ancestors vibrating within me. Their heartbeats joined mine and became one. It was not my body being inspected but the body of an ancient ancestor, a seer, and a warrior. As I reflect the details of my journey in this book, I still remember that my sense of feeling was so heightened that I could feel the breath of the officer upon my naked skin, but at the same time what was happening to me did not feel like it was happening to my body but to another who had taken my place.)

Bend over, spread your legs open. Cough, cough again. Turn around, open your mouth, stick out your tongue, hold up your arms. The officer continued to bark out orders. I and other captives stood helplessly naked before them.

(Within my mind's eye, I had an experience that did not belong to me, but yet had happened to a part of me. In this vision, I was standing on a plank of wood. The ship that delivered me here remained faintly in the background. I was demanded to strip naked again before strangers. My personal-self

desired the tears to flow, hoping they would wash away the shame. It was then that I sensed a powerful embrace that shook my entire body. This embrace released power within me that stopped the tears that were standing ready to embark on the banks of my eyes, and the tears were ushered back. I was strengthened by this embrace, a mental strength that was beyond my human comprehension or ability to exert. This strength would get me through this plane of mental torment. The power of the vibrations of my ancestors subsided. There was a sense of awareness that they were still with me and that my ancestors would guide me through this journey. At this point, I had a knowing that the purpose of imprisonment was more significant than my personal-self and that I am being entrusted with greater mental works, but it is not the personal-self who performs the work. I realized that I am but a temple to move at the direction of the Real-Self within, an observer who must share the truth with those who will soon discover who they are within.)

Captives were not allowed to remain behind the curtain that provided limited privacy as there were so many captives that needed to be examined and processed. A liquid solution was poured over our heads and into our hands. We were ordered to rub the liquid over our skin and our hair and ordered not to shower before authorized. I wondered why the solution was being poured on our bodies. "These fuc---s think we got lice," a captive of color, stated with anger. I think to myself; this stuff is for lice. I don't have lice. Several women, including myself, stood with nothing to cover our nakedness. We stood shivering and waiting for authorization to enter the shower and wash off the very sticky solution. My physical eyes look around the small room. Many captives were being examined. Some were weeping aloud, some were cussing, and others appeared to be familiar with the process, and to expect what was coming next. We are finally demanded to go into the shower and wash off the solution.

"Hurry up and come out of the dam shower," shouted an officer.

An officer distributed an orange pair of pants, socks, boots, panties, a t-shirt, and a sport's bra to each captive. "Get dressed, hurry up," said an officer that seemed to be more agitated than the rest.

After dressing, we were directed to stand in an open area. While I was being held captive in the county jail, and waiting to be sold into the slave prison system, I allowed my hair to be completely dreadlocks. I did not realize this was against prison rules, but only for people of color. Whites only had to bind up their hair from their shoulders. "Get someone from cosmetology," shouted the officer in charge. Looking at me, he said, "you can't have dreadlocks in prison, don't you know that?" shouting as he pointed his finger at me.

I looked at him and said, "No." At this point, I believe that the strength of my ancestors had engulfed me, and the intimidation of officers no longer held power over my mind.

(*I sensed these officers were not yet aware that there is a very thin line between what they believe is a safe place and being enslaved in a system that the officers are helping to perpetuate.*)

The enslaved cosmetologist arrives. She is trying to take down my hair with caution. The skin headed officer screams at her, "cut it, shave it, now!" He ordered. "We don't have all day," shouted the officer. The captive looked at me and mumbled with fear,

"I'm sorry," she said.

"It's ok," I tell her. She starts to shave my head at the top where the dreadlocks were tangled the most while I screamed from the inside. When she finishes, I am bald on the top of my head. I feel so ashamed, but I held my head high.

Newly processed captives were taken to a huge gym where tables were set up around the room to further process captives. These tables were managed by those that, from this point forward, I refer to as Villein. I use the term Villein as this is a term used to describe a class of people who hold the legal status of free persons in all their dealings with all people except their lord. In this case, officers are the Villein of the slave camp, called prison. The word lord will be used to describe the judicial management system, i.e., political, economic, or social order leaders of the system that enslave us.

The Villein directed captives to sit on the bleachers in the gym. Villein had their lunch delivered to them, which consisted of fried chicken, fish, and an array of side dishes. They ate their lunch while we, the captives sat, watched them, and waited. This scene seemed to me to be orchestrated and served as a reminder that as a captive, liberty as we had known it, our constitutional right to liberty is now taken away. After the Villein finished eating, we were finally each handed a brown bag by other captives. The lunch bag contained two molded peanut butter sandwiches and a rotten apple. There was also some very disgusting juice in a cup. I choose not to consume the spoilt food, even as my physical body reminded my mind that it had not been fed.

Villeins were stationed at several tables around the room. These tables served as captives assessment stations. Each captive was called and assessed by a Villein in a particular area, such as but not limited to, mental health, drug addiction, etc. A Villein conducting a mental health assessment with me tried to convince me that it would be to my benefit if I were assessed as needing mental health drugs as this would almost ensure that I would be approved for a mental health monthly check upon release. In addition, "you may find it difficult to sleep in prison without some help," she said.

"I am not, nor have I ever been mentally challenged, and I believe I will sleep just fine," I told her.

After making some written remarks on the paperwork in front of her, she yelled, "Next," and just like that, I was dismissed.

(I choose not to become a victim to mental health drugs. As you follow my truth, you will discover that so many other captives choose this path.)

Once the assessments were complete, each captive was provided with very heavy bunk bed mats made of heavy vinyl. We were also given other related bedding materials and toiletries. "Pick up your things and line up," screamed a Villein. Captives were trying to pick up all the items issued, but could not because the mat was heavy, and there were more things than one's arms or hands could manage to carry. We were not given anything to move the heavy items. "I told you to pick up your things and start moving," screamed the now irritated Villein. A captive that appeared to be around 70 or 75 years of age tried her best to pick up her assigned items. She fell to the floor. "Get up and get moving," screamed the Villein. The captive got up and again was trying to pick up and carry the heavy items. Other captives wanted to assist her, but they were screamed at. "You will not touch anyone else's' belongings, or you will go to lockdown," shouted the Villein. "Do you hear me?" No one said anything, and then the Villein said in a roar, "and your response would be, yes sir!."

The captives with reluctance, followed orders, "yes, sir!" shouted the captives. I only moved my lips, not allowing the vibration of the demanded words to leave my mouth, not that I have ever had an issue with saying yes sir or ma'am as I was taught as a child when addressing my elders. Still, these were not my elders. These were Villein with shaved heads and tattooed arms using their positions as a reminder of what their idea of the good old days was like.

The captive beside me should have followed my lead, but she didn't. Instead, the young captive of color said, "Fu-- this shi-, I ain't saying no fuc---- yes sir to no dam-- body."

The Villein walks over to her, got in her face, so close he could have kissed her. "Inmate, do you have a problem following orders?" said the Villein. The captive rolled her eyes, snatched her head around, and popped her lips, "you heard me," she said. Everything after that exchange happened so quickly, but it seemed as though the events were happening in slow motion. The young captive of color was grabbed, handcuffed, and was taken down on her knees. I am not sure how she was knocked to her knees, but for sure, she did not get down on them willingly as she was kicking and cussing as three Villein took her away.

After the Villein demonstrated to the remaining captives what happens when you disagree with an order, we were ordered to get moving again. I placed my smaller items on top of the mat and started to drag the mat as I could not pick it up. "If you put a hole in that mat, you will be charged for it," said the Villein looking directly at me, I elected to ignore the Villein and continued dragging the mat and items that I had laid on it forward to the dorm where I had been assigned. I reach the hallway of the assigned dorm, C-Hall, but I can't move any further. There are too many captives to count standing in the hallway. They are packed like sardines in a can and sealed tight.

CHAPTER 13

C-Hall OR Mental Ward
Survival OF The Fittest

"Get into your rooms," screamed a Villein. Lee Annandale, or "Alto" as it is known, is the place where female captives are sent for diagnostics. Diagnostics is the place where a captative is supposed to learn to adjust to prison. The Diagnostics camp was filled to capacity. It was apparent to me that captives were not being processed through the diagnostics at any rate of speed as the hall was filled with captives. The room was filled with the thunderous voices of many captives. There was not enough room to move as captives were standing on every spot on the hall. "Get off the hall, or you will not come out of your room for the rest of the day," screamed a Villein. Most of the captives continued talking to each other. They didn't seem to care that the Villein was screaming out demands, from what I witnessed. I sensed fear stare into the room from the eyes of the Villein; however, the captives in the hallway showed no sign of fear. "This entire hall is going on store restriction for the next 30 days if this hall is not cleared right now," screamed the Villein as he turned red in the face. The captives now began to move into their rooms slowly, after which the new captives were able to move through the hallway to locate assigned quarters.

C Hall held approximately 96 captives. Each section in the dorm held four bunk beds, which consisted of eight captives per room. Rooms were jointly clustered in a square that joined sixteen captives. There were two very mildewed and molded bathrooms that were somewhat covered by mildew stained, yellow, worn and torn shower curtain to give one a sense of privacy, and one shower with the same type of worn shower curtain nailed against its doorway. This shower was shared between 16 captives. There was no air conditioning; therefore, windows had to be left open to allow air to flow in.

My first night sleeping in Alto was a strange and restless one. It didn't help that upon waking to go to the restroom. I discovered two captives having their definition of sex in the bathroom stall. I tried to go back to sleep, but sleep now escaped me. Everything was now quiet, but there I lay with my mind awake, and eyes opened. I was prompted from within to look across the room, and there stood a very dark-skinned male encircled with the brightest light staring at me. I felt like I must have fallen asleep and was dreaming. When I realized I was not dreaming, I wanted to scream, but I sensed that all was well. This is one of the Villein, I thought to myself, but the clothes worn by the man in my vision were not the clothes worn by any of the Villein, nor was the encirclement of light that seem to pulsate from around the head. As I continued staring at the male figure, I realized tears were streaming down his face. I was puzzled, and then just like that, the person or my vision faded. I thought to myself, why am I not terrified? Instead, I had such a sense of peace within me. I must have drifted off to sleep because when my eyes opened, it was the next day and time to stand up and be counted by the Villein, who was already screaming, "stand outside your doors for the headcount."

Captives were awakened at 5:00 AM, directed into the hallway to stand by the door of our assigned room for headcount. After the headcount, we went downstairs to the first floor for breakfast. We were told to walk in a straight line down the steps; however, those captives who did not care anything about rules or authority moved as they wished. I noticed that people were jumping when they got to the bottom step, and then I realized why. To reach the dining room or chow hall as some called it, we were required to jump across a huge puddle of water that was gathered at the bottom of the stairs or otherwise wade through it. Those who could not jump had to walk through the sometimes ankle-deep water in order to access the dining area.

I heard the Villein screaming before stepping into the dining hall or chow hall as it was most often called. "Get your tray, sit your a-- down and eat, no talking, let's go," screamed a Villein. It was challenging to eat as flies were everywhere. Captives fanned away flies with one hand and held the plastic spork with the other. A spork is an eating tool that is shaped like a spoon and has small teeth on the opposite end like that were molded like a fork. Captives had to keep up with your spork because it would be at least a year before you were issued another one.

We get into the dining hall, and I notice that the entire dining hall floor is wet. Captives were slipping and falling with their food trays, and Villeins were cursing and screaming. I observed the whole scene, and it stole my appetite. It didn't help that a captive found a worm in their peaches. When the captive informed the Villein of the worm, "take it out, eat, and get out. It's not the first time, and it won't be the last," shouted the Villein. The captive threw the food away and left, most likely still hungry.

I decided not to eat. Instead, an eagerness or a longing within pushed me to desire to learn the history of Alto; therefore, I asked an older captive to share what they knew of the history of the Alto Prison. As soon as the captive started to talk, we were told to shut up, get up, and get out by the Villein. However, the seasoned captive found me later and shared the history of Alto with me.

From this conversation, I discovered that the prison was named after a particular chairman. He was perhaps the chairman of the TB sanitarium. The chairman and his wife were killed in a plane accident. The captive shared that although there is a new addition to the prison, the original area of the prison is dated back to 1926. At that time, the facility was being used as a TB sanitarium. Tuberculosis was thought to be conquered; therefore, the need for the facility lessened, and the facility was turned over to the Georgia Department of Corrections in 1950. It was opened and operated as a prison in 1951. The captive continued speaking, saying that the tuberculosis facility served to treat individuals who were diagnosed with tuberculosis and was constructed with underground tunnels. These tunnels at that time were used to transport the deceased patients to the crematory. These patients had been infected with tuberculosis. It was thought that the bodies of the deceased would contaminate others. The deceased bodies were cremated when there was no one to claim the remains. She stated that the basement contained the crematory for easy access. Also, there was a mound near a water tower on the property of the facility where the ashes of some of those cremated were supposedly buried. I could see the water tower, but was never able to ascertain if the burial mound was there. More than one older captive corroborated this information. She said that once the hospital closed, the entire facility became a prison for men and young males.

As a male prison that is also elected to house young boys, Alto gained a reputation for violence, and by August of 2004, hearings were being held with abundant testimony regarding regular rapes of the most youthful inmates. It was the murder of eighteen-year-old, Wayne Boatwright, Jr., his windpipe crushed after he fought back in a rape that gained attention and eventually, caused the public to demand the prison be closed. Thus, to say Alto has a lot of history that most people would think best be kept hidden away.

I bring this history to your attention in an endeavor to explain what I believe explains for me the energy vibrations I encountered while being held captive there. Captives talked of hearing screams and crying in the night. Most of these events were discharged as sounds being made by other captives, but I knew the vibrations of the sound were more than that. I sensed the struggles, pain, sadness, and the loss of innocent blood that seemed to scream like a howling wind from the walls of the building. The feeling was likened unto the weight of a huge boulder tied to my back, a weight that I was being conditioned to carry.

(Once I accepted my fate and realized it was temporary and that it served a higher purpose that had not yet been revealed, I was honored by my ancestors with more strength and endurance for which I am forever thankful. I now sense the hills, steep valleys, and mountains that await me. Fear had lost its power to

deter me from this journey. I somehow understood that I was not alone in prison! My ancestors were there, guiding and protecting me!)

I estimate that at least 85% of those in Diagnostics are using prescribed and non-prescribed mental health drugs. What I found to be surprising is that many captives were serving a sentence for using drugs, but now, the Villein lords could allow captives to use drugs because they had decided that the drugs they authorized were ok. It was sad to witness how captives ran for the drugs when "pill call" was announced by the Villein. Diagnostics held many captives who were mentally challenged, had viciously murdered others, nonviolent offenders, young, old, and any other category in between, all caged in the same hall and the same room. However, for the approximate 8.5 weeks, I was held captive at Alto, I realized that at least 97 percent of the captives being held in C Hall were economically disadvantaged and highly sedated.

Captives were demanded to perform many duties, including, but not limited to, keeping the entire dorm clean. Responsibilities also included the cleaning up of bowel movements that rained down from captives without the assistance of a toilet to catch the flow. I witnessed that while young captives may not have respected each other, they put forth an effort to respect their elders.

One day a younger captive was assisting an older captive who had just returned from medical to get to her room. When the older captive reached her place, which was direct across from the area, I was housed. I heard a piercing scream. "What the fu-- is that," someone screamed, "oh hel- no," yelled another, the screams became louder, and I rose from the bunk to look across the hall to see what was going on, but before my eyes could see, a scent that smelled like a three-day-old spoiled meat hit my nostrils like a force of strong wind, and then remained there, circling around, and haunting me, causing me to choke. The smell not only attacked me but attacked everyone in the dorm. People were running and holding their noses because of the foul smell. The young captive who had walked the now terrified, and soiled captive to the dorm was trying to take off her now stained boots as she cussed at the situation. Even on reflection, I can still sense the awful smell. It seems that medical had given the captive a potent laxative known by and referred to by captives as the "Green Monster." The problem is that medical failed to explain to the older captive what the Green Monster was capable of and that she had only twenty minutes to make it to the restroom. The captive had walked slowly back to the dorm, as she was an older woman, and the walk was at least two blocks. You guessed it! The captive's bowels escaped before she could make it to the restroom.

When the Villein determined what had happened, they demanded captives to clean up the feces, and then they ran from the dorm leaving the captives behind. I did not participate in the cleanup, I tried to locate a place to hide from the smell, but there was no place of escape as the foul smell took the entire dorm hostage. Not only did medical not tell her what to expect regarding the powerful laxative, but they also did not tell her that she needed to remain on the toilet as her bowels would continue to flow for a while. After the initial clean up on "the isle across the hall" was completed by captives who tied shirts around their faces in an effort to block the foul smell that continued attacking everyone. The woman started walking around in the room in which she was housed, and the entire drama started over again as the Green Monster was not yet finished moving through her. She walked in the feces and tracked it throughout the hall. At this point, the woman who I learned was mentally challenged, became afraid, and began running around asking for help to make her bowels stop. As the loosed bowels flowed from her and traveled around the dorm on the bottom of her shoes, and on the shoes of everyone who ran from the room to escape, captives started banging on the exit door to be let out of the dorm, but the Villein had left the hall and were nowhere to be found.

This behavior was prominent throughout Diagnostics as it relates to Villeins. Medical served the drugs and the Villein didn't seem to care.

CHAPTER 14

Killing Captives Softly With Meds

One morning, captives were screaming for the assistance of a Villein. The cry for help awakened me from my sleep. "I think she had a stroke; she can't talk, her mouth is twisted, and she is slobbering," screamed a captive. "Please get medical," cried a captive. I witnessed that it took the medical team about an hour or more to arrive. Later during the week, when I spoke to the captive, I could see that her mouth was twisted. She told me that the medical team had given her the wrong pills. She said that she was still not feeling well and had gone back to medical but was told by medical that they believed she was pretending to be ill, and if she continued to fill out sick call slips to be seen at medical, she would be taken to lockdown. She also revealed to me that the medical told her that the incorrect medicine would wear off soon; this was not an isolated incident as I was also given the wrong medicine.

The process for receiving over the counter medicine is that all captives who are prescribed meds go to a medical distribution hall where a medical Villein distributes the medicine. The officer Villein stands to watch to check the captive's mouth to ensure they swallow the medication. However, this is often missed as captives sell their medicines to the highest bidder. The medical Villeins are rushed because there are so many captives on prescribed drugs, and time is limited. I stand in line, awaiting my turn to receive medicine for hypertension. I notice that the pill given to me by the Medical Villein is a different color than the one I had been given previously and alert the medical Villein of the difference. "This is your prescription, it's just a different color," said the medical Villein. Intuition alerted me not to take the pills handed to me, but the Villein officer rushed me. I placed the tablets in my mouth and drank the water to wash them down. Thirty minutes after taking the pill, I became very dizzy, and my steps were unbalanced. My stomach started having an involuntary spastic movement, and I discharged everything that I had consumed, afterward, I felt better. I decided to see if I was given that same pill the next morning. When I was given a different color, I explained to the Medical Villein that I was given a different colored pill the day before. In addition, I communicated to her the side-effects as a result of digesting the pill the day before. "It is your responsibility to make sure you take the correct pill," we do make mistakes, she said. I think to myself, but you are the medical personnel, and you are providing me the pill. I realize at that moment that I must be meticulous and cannot trust the medicines I am being offered. As captives in Diagnostics, we were at the mercy of the Villein. We could not contact our families because our phone list and even our financial requests would not be approved for 30-45 days.

(In other words, we could not call for outside assistance from our families or anyone else.)

CHAPTER 15

Making of the Mafia Environment

New captives being processed through diagnostics would not be given the authorization to call home or even have individuals authorized to place money on their books for 30 to 45 days. Imagine someone who has never seen the inside of a jail witnessing individuals dying, and committing suicide, but not being able to speak with their loved ones. As a captive in prison diagnostics, you are not allowed to talk to your family for several weeks. It would take this long to get a captive's phone number approved. A captative's family is required to send in a copy of their birth certificate, social security card, and other personal information that most seasoned individuals do not wish to divulge, especially to the State of Georgia. As a result of this convoluted process, many captives are not able to have individuals financially approved to place funds on their books. Therefore, these captives are subject to finding alternative means to make a phone call to their family or having funds made available for them to use.

I was worried that my family would not know where I had been taken. I finally speak to another captive who had empathy for me as she had gone through what I was going through. She provided me with a 3-way call that allowed me to speak with my daughter so that I could let her know where I had been taken. Look for the word "Hell" in the dictionary, and you will most likely discover a picture of Alto, aka Slave Camp. The rules captives endured were designed by Villein lords. These rules subjected every captive to a mafia-type system.

Captives not yet financially approved to have family or others place money on their books could not purchase items from the store. These items included hygiene items that captives would need. Captives in the general population and some in Diagnostics who were already finically approved benefited from this rule. Thus a mafia-type system is engineered and administered by the captives.

The mafia-type system within the prison slave camp allowed captives who were not yet financially approved to purchase items from the prison store on the books of those captives who were financially approved. Captives in diagnostics would have their family put money on the books of a financially approved captive in the general population. The captive in the general population would then take the Diagnostic captive's order and have it delivered. Captives in Diagnostics used their connection to those in the general community to buy from the store and sell the items at a higher price to financially unapproved captives in Diagnostics who did not have connections. Captives in Diagnostics, by slave camp rules, were not allowed to associate with captives in the general population. What I could not understand is how the captives in diagnostics received the items purchased since we were not able to associate with the captives in the general population and were housed separately. Then one night, I heard a male's voice, "be ready, he's on the way," the voice said. I pretended to be asleep, and within minutes, I heard the door opened between the diagnostics and the general population and witnessed a

Villein handoff two large bags of store products to a diagnostics captive. I could not believe what I had just witnessed. Villein, who threatened, screamed, and hauled captives off to lockdown for nothing more than speaking, were playing a role in the mayhem being inflicted at Alto. As I drifted off to sleep, I realized that all were not as they seemed to be.

"Inmates get up, get dressed. Let's go," said the Villein. "You did not stand for a Lieutenant, so you will march in the rain until you remember to stand to your feet for your superiors," screamed the Villein. I thought to myself, march in the rain? We were not even issued a raincoat or even a coat. We were asleep, We didn't know a Lieutenant was in the hall, and this is Sunday, it's supposed to be a down day. A captive, raising her voice with a hint of anger, shouted among the others visibly angry but silent captives. "Oh! You are speaking for everyone, step out of the line inmate," said the Villein. The captive steps out of the lineup of captives. "Sir, permission to speak, sir," requested the captive. "No inmate, you will not speak, but you will go to lockdown. Cuff her," the Villein said to a lowered ranking Villein. The captive was handcuffed and carried to lockdown. Before we were dismissed to go out into the rain without a coat to march, we were reminded that if one captive violates a rule, every captive is held responsible. Captives moaned, but it seemed that no one else was willing to risk being taken to the lockdown that day. Intuitively, I understood this was not a place to exercise your constitutional right of free speech, but observe the system at work, play the game, and live to fight another day.

(In this place, the Villein held the rules of the game and changed them at their leisure. Captives were the spoil, and justice was nowhere to be found.)

In prison, one faces captives with mental health challenges, mafia-type operating systems, and overcrowding within the dorms. Injustice is poured out by the Villein like hot burning flames upon captives and causes hostilities to coat the facility like a fresh coat of paint. Every captive seemed to be seeking to establish some personal barrier for their protection. When a Villein or another captive penetrated this seemingly invisible barrier, there was always trouble. I observed that the mentally challenged captives seemed to explode more than others.

A young captive who seemed to have mental challenges, who could barely speak a coherent sentence, was angered because another captive did not provide her prison store food items to her after money was placed on the book of the financially approved captive for that purpose. The young angered captive whose weight appeared to be around 350 plus pounds pulled off all her clothes except her sports bra, and panties, the panties looked from the back like a G-string on her. One could only see a white strip of cloth separating her butt cheeks. The huge captive jumped on a captive who appeared to weigh around 125 pounds. The huge captive was screaming the entire time as she was hitting her with closed fists, "I want my fuc---- sh--," and was committed to beating the captive and anyone who tried to interfere. Before officer Villein could stop the fight, well, it was not really a fight, it was a beat down, and the huge captive had bitten off the end of the other captive's finger. Villein thought the scene was comical as they handcuffed and dragged the huge captive down the hall, wearing only her sports bra and panties. "Were you hungry?" The Villein chuckled and joked as they dragged the huge captive face down and bottom-up through the hallway, taking her to the lockdown. Medical transported the other captive and the tip of her finger. Perhaps the finger was eaten as I never saw it again.

Chapter 16

Rehabilitation in Prison is the Illusion
A Trained Mind is the Solution

Rehabilitation in prison is an illusion. If your mind was not trained or evolving before you were captured, it most likely would continue to devolve unless one retrained his or her mind, and there was a change in mental direction. Most captives did not have trained minds and did not seek to be awakened; therefore, they vibrated from the lower instinctive mind only. Observing the prison slave system, I realized that prison exists for the same purpose and motive as the slave plantations, which is weaving a complex system of separation that destroys generations. These generations allow the system to become the dictatorship of those not yet woke as well as those yet to be captured. You see, the system that was established mandating that captives' families be financially approved before being able to put money on a captive's books caused captives to look for other means to get what they believed they needed. It appeared that the established system caused a greater problem, but was the system the problem? My ancestors, who had now begun to have a stronger presence within me, were guiding and directing me to focus more internally. It is for this reason that I can say, "No," to the question of, "did the system cause the greater problem?" The system is not and will never be the problem, although it was established as an illusion that appears to be the problem. The truth is that there is no problem, only a solution. The solution lies within every captive and even those not captured. I comprehended that I had to work on myself as I had inner currents that needed to vibrate and flow without obstruction.

(I am not suggesting that some people do not belong in prison, but I will say that from what I have seen, most of the individuals in prison have a psychological challenge. Mental illness must be addressed in the prison system. Prescribing heavy medication for those with mental illness is not the solution.)

CHAPTER 17

The Awakening

As I assessed my situation, I recognized two urgent matters that I needed to rectify as I began to awaken. The Villein had cut and shaved my head, and I was experiencing an inferiority complex about not having my covering. I also desired to become acquainted with other strong captives who were awakened or were already woke. I met a captive who wore a beautiful scarf, and I desired one to cover my crown. "How can I get a scarf," I asked the captive? "I am a Muslim, I wear a hijab," she corrected me. "The only way you will be granted authority to wear a hijab in here is that you are Muslim," she stated. As I pondered this information, I decided to become a Muslim as this would allow me to be a part of what I thought were some powerful women, and of course, I could wear a hijab to cover my naked head. It didn't take long to join the ranks of the Muslims and be authorized to wear the hijab, but the powerful women I sought were not within the ranks. The bitterness directed at each other within the group of female Muslims was like the falling of leaves to the ground at the commencing of Autumn. There were so many of them, but they had fallen, laying on the earth, covering each other, and being trampled. I thought to myself if only these beautiful women would realize that they have fallen not to fertilize the soil in Pulaski, but to rise and use their power to make a difference.

By the fourth meeting, there was a loud argument by the Muslim sisters that was a breath away from being a full-fledged fight. I assessed my situation like this, at least I get to wear the hijab, but I did not desire to be a part of the problem as I was seeking solutions. I never attended another Islamic meeting at the Alto Slave Camp. As I pondered my decision not to attend another Islamic meeting, I was alerted to the fact that here I was again seeking an external solution. My ancestors reminded me that all the answers lie within. When would I understand that all the solutions I sought were never going to be external? I decided to ponder the question, "what is the solution that I seek? But beyond that, what is the question that I need to ask?"

As I finally settled on the bunk bed, lying on a mattress that felt like I was sleeping on rocks, I began to drift off to sleep. I was in a place between sleep and being awake. I was determined to disengage my thoughts from the adverse events of the day. This included the fight and the argument at the Islamic meeting and many others that my mind seemed to want to hold on to. Going within, I willed my mind to stop thinking about the loss of my hair and to think of gratifying thoughts that I now realize are a part of me in the oneness of the universe. I reflected on the untrained minds of captives who believed they had no choice other than to use violence to settle conflicts, and how I could introduce information that may serve to retrain the minds of the captives. I thought about how some captives were entwined by religious values that served to keep them bound in false hope. I think to myself, what is the underlying problem? The response to my question appeared within my mind like a cloud against a light blue sky.

I could clearly see the system that we believed we were being forced to exist in. A system that our mind presented to us is fueled by deceit and injustice. A system we believe underserved already infuriated captives with more bitterness, a system that we believe offers no hope A system that serves to snatch away, in so many cases, thirty-plus years of liberty from human beings. The system that I am describing is a system that has passed laws that seem to ensure nepotistic rights to the future heirs of Villein and their lords. I had never seen the system from the inside before, and what I see now, caused me to scream from the inside. As I observed the system, I realized that I played a part in creating the system that my physical body is not captured within.

Being ushered deeply into the lucid dream State of being awake and asleep, I felt so at peace. I imagined this would be the feeling of nothingness. Time seemed to have stepped back and stood still as I observed a scene as one who had not yet been noticed. However, I had a knowing that the stage had been set for my observation. I sensed a strong presence of my ancestors once again becoming my guiding light. In the vision, I could see the man of tears; this was the same man of tears from my previous vision upon my first night of stay at Alto. There was a vast table positioned in the middle of a huge room, and something was lying in the center of the table. The table was stationed between the man of tears and another man. The other man seemed to be molded from pure physical strength. He had powerful looking arms and legs and was very tall. There were Villein and lords present, and a great crowd of witnesses surrounded the vast table. The man of tears and the strong man jumped on the top of the massive table at the same time. It seemed to me that a gush of air propelled them each upon the table. The man of tears who was very small in stature, after jumping on the table, remained as still as a star against the dark of the night. But the strong man stepped to the man of tears and began to physically attack him as the crowd of witnesses looked on. I wanted to cover my eyes, but could not. It seemed like the strong man was beating the man of tears for centuries. I thought the abuse would never end, and as much as I wanted to close my eyes, I was compelled to continue to watch the scene. I watched as the life flickered and then went silent as it was snatched from the man of tears by the strong man. The only evidence that life ever existed in the man of tears were the illuminated tears that streamed down his now expressionless face. Even though the man of tears seemed lifeless, I sensed he was speaking with me through thought. I could not hear the thoughts of the man of tears, for his words vibrated clearly within me. "Your thoughts are more powerful. The strong man has no power over your Real Self. Fear and entanglement is an illusion." I had no idea what those words meant, but my mind placed them in a mental file. As the vision continued, and the voice within became silent, the faces of the great crowd of witnesses were smiling even as they hung their heads. I thought to myself, why are they smiling? One of the lords in the vision walked to the table and picked up the object from the center of the table and presented it to the strong man. It appeared to me to be a huge chunk of meat. Within my being, I heard a vibration and understood the vibration that, for me, became words. (***"Do not be confused, my daughter. Systems established for your ancestors are now more advanced, but you are here and shall know the truth. Observe, and you will gain an understanding of what must be done at the right time."***) I thought to myself, "Is this the response to my question?" My mind remained confused regarding the scene before me. After what seemed liked hours, I opened my eyes only to discover; I had only been meditating for about twenty minutes. I was not sure what to do about the vision that was shared with me, but I remembered my ancestors indicated the "right time." I assumed when the right time arrived, I would know, until then, I would go on observing and being.

I continued to invest my time in exercising and studying books of the ancients. I worked out, meditated, learned the rules, and talked with captives who wanted to share their journey with me.

Chapter 18

Trapped by the Villein...Released by Another

One day I was standing in the adjoining room looking out of the window and enjoying a cool breeze that was flowing in. I remember watching the cars moving down the roadway, listening to the sound of freedom as I had once known it. I was unaware that the headcount of the captives had been called. We were counted several times a day. Counting individuals, this often baffled me, like where are we going to run? Regardless, we were counted like clockwork every day. A captive is required to be standing at a specific place when they are being counted. On that day, I was not in the right place, and time had escaped me. I heard a captive whisper, "count, Ms. Spell." I turned around and saw the most aggressive and heartless Villein at the prison slave camp staring at me. My heart wanted to leap out and run away, but like a calm sea, my mind held my body still. Within seconds, I felt in control of my physical body. I then turned to go back through the open doorway to the area I was assigned to, but the two Villein blocked me, one directly behind me, and the other one stood in the doorway blocking my way. I was sandwiched between them. Inmate, "what is the question," screamed the Villein behind me at the top of his voice, screaming directly in my ears until my ears rang. My physical body wanted to urinate as fear beat at my heart, screaming to enter. However, my mind focused on the strength of my ancestors before me, and courage took control. I could sense fear slithering back to its origin, even as the Villein continued to scream as if I was hard of hearing. The Villein kept screaming the same question over and over, and I continued to quietly stand where I was as I could not get through the doorway. The Villein officers had not taught me the password. The Villein in front of me started laughing, but the Villein behind me, who was still screaming at me to say the password began to cough uncontrollably. This Villein began to cough and could not stop. He turned red, and it seemed to me he was chocking. I did not look back. I continued to focus on the courage and the guidance of my ancestors.

Finally, the Villein blocking me realized that the other Villein was under some coughing attack and said to the coughing Villein, "she does not know the password." They both walked away with one of the Villein turning strawberry red, and still coughing as loud as he had screamed. The next day I heard that the two Villein had compromised their positions and were relocated. I never understood how they compromised their jobs, but I never saw the two Villein again, and within a week, I was sold and was being delivered to the slave camp at Pulaski State Prison.

Before being transported from Alto, in fact, on the same day that I became a target of the two Villein who was said to have comprised their positions, two skinhead Cert Villein came to the hall where I was housed. My name was called loudly, and then all the captives started assisting in the call of my name. Captives did this to ensure that one heard when they were being called. I thought to myself, what now? I came out of the room and approached the two Villeins. "You need to come with us," said one of the Villeins. "Let's go," they said. I am led out of the dorm door to the outside. It is a very chilly morning, and it is raining. Both Villeins wore raincoats to protect them. I had nothing to protect me from the elements as we were not issued a parka in diagnostics. I walked behind the Villein, cold and getting wetter by the moment, having no idea of where I was being taken.

We finally reach the main office; we walk inside the room, and another man is standing there. I am confused about what was happening. I think perhaps I am being summoned because I was not standing by my assigned bunk for the headcount. The man that is standing in the room opens his mouth and speaks. "You are…" and says my name. I respond with "yes." "You have been served," said the man in the room. Before even looking at the document, I realized the man is a Process Server, and what I had just received was divorce papers, signed and sealed by the man who I married for better, for worse, in sickness and poverty. Then why was I surprised? After all, I was in the Troup County Jail when he said to me, **"I did not sign up for this."**

After I was served with the divorce papers, the two Villeins immediately began to walk me back to the dorm. I am walking fast because it is cold and it is still raining. As I am moving at a fast pace, I feel the need to allow the deeply buried tears to be released. You see, in the rain, I would be able to disguise the tears as the rain upon my face. My instinctive mind is screaming from the inside, "you are all alone now!" My physical body began to feel very heavy, so heavy that I had to slow my pace of walking. When my steps were slowed, I sensed that my physical body and my mind began to appreciate the rain. I experienced a calmness surrounding me. I imagined that the rainwater was washing away the past, and just like that, I started to smile. Through the strength of my ancestors, I could survive another day. I knew they were with me. I willed my intellectual mind to assess my present situation. I smiled because I realized that I would never miss what I had never had with this person and that what I never had was true love. I understood at that moment that the universe, my Creator, the Absolute were granting me the favor to release all past karma that had not served for my higher purpose. *I realized that "Nothing just happens."* With this new perspective, I look forward to the next lesson on the prison camp path.

CHAPTER 19

Sold July 17, 2017
To the Highest Bidder
Pulaski State Prison

Several captives were taken to the transport area of Lee Annandale or Alto along with me. We were all being processed to be sent to a new slave camp. The head transport Villein reminded me of the house slave in the movie Jango, but a hundred times worse. "Get your as-es in here, shut the fu-- up, what the fu—are you looking at," screamed the transport Villein as he verbally shouted out orders, attempting to intimidate and torment the captives. This Villein had each captive line up and then proceeded to walk down the line, verbally attacking each of us. When he got to me, he stopped. "Oh, you are one of the proud ones hun' convict," he snickered, moving closer to me. I look at him in the eyes, "yes, I am proud, and everyone in prison is not guilty, sir," I said, responding to his remarks of "inmates not being mad at him as we put ourselves in prison." He moves closer to me and whispers in my ear, "you lost every right when you got locked up, and in here, you are guilty," he said. I looked at him and realized that he was a pawn of illusion being used by the system. I realized he was an actor in the play that I had unintentionally created.

Therefore, intellectually, I reasoned that the comment did not warrant a response as this actor was vibrating from a lower frequency. He walked away from me with a facial smirk that, in my opinion, made him believe he had won or scored one for his team.

After the Villein completed his attempt to humiliate us, he demanded that we all enter a small cage where we were locked in and sat on benches. The other Villein searched through our belongings, taking panties, t-shirts, and anything else they decided they wanted to take on the State's behalf. While we waited, we were given brown paper bags that held two peanut butter sandwiches and an apple. The sandwiches had to be returned several times as the bread was green, and the peanut butter molded. Finally, the Villein just gave up on feeding us a meal that was spoiled and told us to eat at our own risk. I ate the apple; it was the only item that seemed edible. Some captives were so hungry that they scraped the mold off the peanut butter, broke the green parts off the bread, and ate. We were given beige pants and a shirt to replace the orange uniforms and finally ushered outside to be handcuffed, shackled, and loaded in the vehicle for transport.

The aggressive male transport Villein chooses to shackle and handcuff me. I could not understand why a female Villein was not available to shackle me as they had done the other captives, yet I remained silent and observed the scene. We were demanded to face the wall with our arms and legs spread apart. As the transport Villein reached his arms around my waist, I could feel the tips of his fingers lightly brush against the nipples of my breast, and I contemplated saying something to the female Villein who was standing not far away. No, be quiet, I told myself, you will cause PREA to become involved, and you will stay here in the lockdown, pending an investigation.

Keeping my mouth closed about what the Villein had done, I got into the vehicle and moved to the back and sat down. The transport Villein, who had violated my space and my body looked in the vehicle and caught my glance. I looked at him in the eyes to let him know that I was aware of the physical violation. He held my glance, and I was positively aware with a knowing that he knew that I knew his touch was intentional. His glance screamed because I can! I held my head high, turned away from him, and focused on what was important, "survival." Reserve my mental strength for the fight that was approaching.

After traveling for what seemed like many hours, we arrive at the prison slave camp, called Pulaski State Prison. I saw numerous female Villein of color and hoped that conditions would not be as oppressive as the ones I had just left at Alto. Right away, we encountered "I ain't your Mama" body language and attitudes that screamed, convicts from the female Villein of color. Pulaski has beautifully landscaped yards, thanks to the captives, but within the walls was mass confusion. I was grateful that at least they had carts to place the mattress and other personal items that were assigned to captives. Intake at Pulaski was simplified as captives had already been fully inspected at Alto.

My wrist was sore after being tightly handcuffed, and I just wanted to go somewhere and rest; however, captives had to wait. It seems that Pulaski did not have any available beds. As new captives, we had to wait until Pulaski could make the necessary bed arrangements. Finally, I was processed in and escorted by a Villein to a building defined as E4. The dorm within the building was much cleaner than Alto, and I thought to myself, not home, but better than Alto diagnostics. There were only two beds in the room, a toilet with a half door, which was a welcomed change. The person I was placed in the room with seemed ok. She had the same first name as me. After I put my things away, I went to call my family to let them know where I had been taken. As I walked into the lobby, I saw Liza, the co-defendant. I was shocked that I would be placed in the same dorm with a person who lied against me to save herself. She must have been surprised or fearful because the next day, a Villein came into the room where I was housed. "Ms. Spell, pack your things, we need to move you, your co-defendant is in this dorm," she stated.

"I know it. I have already seen her. I don't have a hidden agenda regarding her, and as far as I am concerned, she does not exist," I said to the Villein.

"She was here first, so we have to move you," said the Villein. I was asked to pack up for the move. I packed my things and prepared for relocation. Again, there were not any available beds. I remained packed up and waiting to be moved for hours. Finally, two Villein came to escort me to another dorm. I had no idea where I was being taken.

I was disappointed about having to relocate within the prison slave camp walls so soon. As we moved slowly down the sidewalks, pushing the cart that held the belongings issued to me by the State, following the Villein, they were snickering as they discussed with each other a particular person that was housed in the room where they were taking me. Looking at me, a Villein said, "she's worried about being moved, she should be praying that a big girl doesn't cause the top bunk to fall on her," and then they broke out with loud laughter. They talked about the environment I would be entering, and each step caused me to feel like I wanted to run away. Responding to the statement of the Villein, I asked, "are the bed bunks style?" "One of the beds is. The one you are assigned to, and you are on the bottom and fatso is in the top bunk," said the laughing Villein. "How many beds are in the room, I ask?" "Three," said one of the Villein. The Villein now projected body language that said, stop asking questions. I remained silent for the remaining part of the walk.

On the way to the dorm, we were approached by a management Villein who seemed to be inspecting me. She asked why I was looking so sad. The officer Villein told her that I did not want to be moved. The management Villein looked at me and said, "I handpicked you for E7, and you don't want to move there?" I did not know what to say. I just said, "thank you," and we continued walking.

I was taken to dorm E7, which was across the compound. At the time, it seemed blocks away from E4. We arrived, and as I entered the building, I saw wheelchairs and walkers lined up against the walls in the halls. The entire dorm smelled of urine and other terrible smells. A captive who had been standing by the window looking out when we arrived began cussing as soon as the Villein stepped foot inside the door. She seemed to be upset because she was not allowed to attend a July 4th celebration that was being held on the compound. The two Villein that transported me to the dorm ignored the verbally abusive captive. Looking around the halls of the dorm, I thought to myself, **"I will not grow old in this place."** I realized a feeling of sadness coming over me as I preferred not to be in what I understood to be the medical dorm. It appeared to me to be a graveyard, a place where captives are taken to die. Then I remembered the sentence that was handed down by the judge, 50 years, do 20. I dismissed this thought and replaced that thought with another, I say to my mind, "I will not do 20 years in this place."

I am taken to a room on "C Hall." Can you believe it, another "C-Hall?" The two other captives that shared the room were not there. They were at the 4th of July celebration. I was told earlier that I would be assigned to the bottom bunk, but upon entering the tiny room, the Villein realized that the bottom bunk was taken. The Villein seems to be confused and called someone to determine if the bottom bunk was assigned. You guessed it, the captive that the Villein was laughing about the entire trip had assigned herself to the bottom bunk. Well, you can just about imagine the welcome I received when she returned from the 4th of July celebration and discovered she had to move back to the top bunk, and yes, this made it very difficult for me.

Because I did not plan to transcend in prison, my family and supporters hired what I thought was an appeal attorney. In this next chapter, you will read about that illusion.

Chapter 20

The Illusion of The Savior Attorney

While in captivity in Troup County, my family and I secured another attorney to handle my appeal. When I say family, I speak of my children who gave of their resources and also of people who did not know me. They graciously contributed money to help pay for my attorney fees. The attorney we chose had raving reviews posted on the internet. *Attorneys are part of the delusion that we call a justice system. They are like a rope that connects one to a weak branch. We have no idea that the branch will not hold us. We do not know that it will fail us. The rope is only an illusion of security, and it can not hold or protect you.*

It is July 2017; I had gone to trial in March, and I had not yet been provided with a copy of my trial transcripts. The new attorney had not bothered to contact me regarding my court appeal even though he was obtained several months before. We will observe this picture later as we progress further into the prison slave camp.

CHAPTER 21

Too Close for Comfort

The room where I would be detained for the next five months was way too small for three people; the room had a set of bunk beds and a single bed next to it. The beds were perhaps a foot apart. There was no ladder to climb onto the top bunk, and many captives fell and severely hurt themselves as a result of trying to climb onto the high bunk bed. The three of us could not move around the room at the same time. If an emergency had occurred, it would have been challenging to exit the room safely.

The captive introducing herself as the "Dorm Orderly" took it upon herself to train me in the survival skills of the prison, and for this, I will be forever grateful. The Dorm Orderly seemed to be proud of her unsalaried position. I soon discovered that she was the person that wrote letters to management Villein to have a captive removed from the dorm when the captive did not meet her expectations.

I had been getting up around 6:00 AM to prepare for my day, which included brushing my teeth, as well as attending to other hygiene matters. On the third morning of my arrival, I was standing at the sink, brushing my teeth. The sink was in the same room with the three beds.

There was no escaping the sounds of running water or a toothbrush scraping against one's teeth as they brushed or even the roaring flush of the toilet in this one-size-fits-all room. The captive with the oversized butt became very irritated with me. "Look, you are going to have to brush your teeth quieter, why are you up so early, this shi- ain't gonna work," she stated loudly with a voice that oozed irritation. I did not say anything to this captive as I had previously observed that she was upset with me for having been moved to the top bunk. She continues, "did you hear me talking to you?"

I turn from the sink where I was standing looking up at her as she lay in the top bunk, I ask her, "what would she have me to do since I need to brush my teeth?" Even as I asked her the questions, I was trying to figure out in my head how a person could brush quietly.

"I don't give a fu— what you do, but you will not get up at 6:00 in the morning and disturb me," said the captive with the oversized butt.

The Dorm Orderly, who shared the room with us, had minutes before brushed her teeth and had left the room. Nothing was said to her about brushing her teeth. Therefore, I understood this captive was not upset about the brushing of teeth; she was still angry with me because she believed I took the bottom bunk from her. I decided to ignore her, but this only infuriated her more. She now sits up in the bed and begins to hurl profanity at me. I was shocked and was not sure of what to do. I grabbed my shirt off the bottom bunk and decided to locate the Dorm Orderly for direction.

When I walk out of the room, the oversized butt captive comes down from the top bed, slams the door, and locks me out of the room. I located the Dorm Orderly and communicated to her what just occurred, including being locked out of the room. The dorm orderly did not seem to want to get involved, but I gave her no choice. She knocked on the door, and the oversized butt captive opened it. "What's going on, said the dorm orderly?"

"You need to tell this bit— how to act in a room. She is disturbing my sleep and then tries to get smart with me," screamed oversized butt. Oversized butt then looks directly at me and says, "I started to kick you in your fuck---face."

I can't believe what I am hearing, another human being contemplating kicking another in their face because of the person merely brushing their teeth. I look at her and say in a monotone voice, but at the same time, intending to let her know that I was not, and would not be intimidated, and I say to her, "that would have been a mistake."

She then starts to scream at me more loudly while at the same time hurling profanity. She walks into the hallway, where she has a captive audience and begins to tell everyone her account of what she believes occurred. I remain in the room; after all, I am the new person. The new person must earn allies, and allies seemed to be gained through the providing of food and other resources. I had no intention of winning allies in that manner. I finished getting dressed so that I would be inspection ready. Each captive had to have their assigned quarters cleaned and be fully dressed by 8:00 AM, which is when each captive is again counted. If captives were not inspection ready, they were subject to receiving a Derogatory Report or DR as it is defined.

I discovered that a Dorm Orderly is one who tells on everyone else, or at least most captives believe that they did. In my case, I was glad for the snitch orderly, as she wrote a letter to the Villein unit manager and divulged what had occurred between me and the captive with the huge butt. On the same day of the occurrence, I had also written a letter to the same management Villein stating that I had been threatened by the captive with the huge butt. Later that week, I had gone out for an appointment. Upon my return to the dorm, I discovered that the oversized butt captive had been relocated to another dorm. This had only taken three days. I was elated as I did not wish to close my eyes around a person who had already threatened to kick me in my face.

What I did not know is that my family had contacted the prison to tell them that they would be observing. They wanted the prison camp to see that I had support on the outside.

(For those who may not know how important this is, please understand it is vitally important. One must demonstrate to the prison slave camp that the captive has someone on the outside who cares; otherwise, that captive may not be receiving adequate medical attention and is often treated with contempt.)

Chapter 22

Moving in the Flow of Prison Slave Camp

My stay in the medical dorm was challenging because there were ill captives everywhere. They were not only ill physically, but they were also mentally challenged, and most often, physical and mental illness were the predicaments of the same captive. Some captives were in wheelchairs and walkers, twisted and curved over so severely to the point that their feet where the only thing they could see with no effort. Some were so medicated that they would fall and bust their head open constantly, and some others just slept most of the time. Then, there were some that you wish would sleep, because they were always agitated with everyone. You had those who could not feel when they were going to have a bowel movement, which caused the entire dorm to run for cover. Finally, you had those who tried to bully anyone they thought was weaker, and there was a lot of room for a captive with that mindset to operate.

The officer Villeins at Pulaski State Prison were as different as night and day from those at Alto. Most of Alto officer Villeins were white skinheads. The majority of those at Pulaski were from the Black Nation. I noticed that the older officer Villeins at Pulaski prison operated from an attitude of "I ain't your Mama. The younger officer

Villein displayed a sense of understanding and had more empathy for the captives; however, you could never be sure of what attitude you were going to encounter.

My first encounter with a Villein team identified as "The Cert Team" was an embarrassing one for me. E7, which is the dorm I was housed in, was called out to lunch; this was my first encounter with Cert as well as my first trip to the dining hall. "My Bunkie," this is a term used to refer to another captive sharing a room, and this term is only used if one respects the person sharing the room; otherwise, the term used is, "that bit—in my room." Anyway, my Bunkie, the dorm orderly, and my self-designated trainer had gone to the dining hall, sometimes referred to as "chow hall" to eat. We were served fresh apples; I was so excited to be served apples as I could not eat the awful food that was served on the dirty hard plastic trays. I am given extra apples. My Bunkie and four others did not want their apples, so I gladly accepted them. I planned to take the apples back to the room and eat them later. I did not realize that there was a rule against carrying food back to the dorm (unlike Alto) It made sense to me that we could take items such as apples back to the dorm, but I was wrong about this. I started to walk out of the dining hall with the apples in my hand.

"You can't walk out with the apples in your hand like that, you have to hide them," said my Bunkie. "Put them in your bra," she said. I put the apples in my bra. "No, not like that; they will be seen," she said, laughing.

By this time, I am already at the door and say, "it will be ok. I don't think anyone will care. We took the food back to the dorm at Alto."

I walked out of the dining hall door and saw an officer Villein and decided to go another way. The dining hall holds about 120 people, so there are a lot of captives on the walk. When I turn to go in another direction, I walked directly in front of a member of the Cert team, but Cert did not notice that I have extra breasts when there should be only two. I clear Cert and walk directly into the Deputy Warden, who does notice that I have extra breasts. Speaking in a loud tone, she asks, "what do you have up there?" She then calls Cert to come over to investigate. Cert walks over from where I had just passed them and became visibly upset that I just caused them to look bad in front of not only the Deputy Warden, but the Warden was also present. While everyone is waiting behind me to move, captives are not allowed to walk when a management Villein is on the walk until authorized. Cert demanded that I remove whatever I was hiding in my breast area; therefore, one by one, I removed each apple from my body storage. When I removed the fourth apple, the six feet eight-inch Villein Cert team member said, "How many apples do you have?"

I try to stretch my 5'2" body to look the Villein Cert officer in the face. That was not going to happen, so I responded, saying, "just a few, I was going to save them for dinner."

"For dinner! We are going to give you dinner," said the Cert Villein. I wanted to tell her that if dinner would be anything like lunch that I would pray, she let me keep my apples, but she took the apples from me and whispered, "you made me look bad in front of the Warden." Laughter roared from the captives who had witnessed the scene as I am released to continue walking. I decided that day that I would not transport food from the dining hall ever again, even if it had been given to me. I felt terrible that I caused the Villein Cert officer to look bad. The Cert team Villeins were supposed to be mean and hard, but I found Cert members to treat captives with more respect than most of the Villein officers. Cert team members at the Pulaski prison did not seem to have the old school Willie Lynch System syndrome.

Looking back, I realize that it was not age that made a difference in a Villein attitude. It was the number of years a Villein had served. It appeared that those who had served five years or more as an officer or in any other capacity were most often more odious. Working as an officer for over several years may explain the Villein's attitude in dorm E7.

The officer Villein, responsible for the security of E7 which is considered the medical dorm, was very loud, hurled profanity all day, gossiped about captives, was unprofessional and showed favoritism to those who demonstrated the same characteristics. She was young but had been an officer for more than five years. Her demeanor was so bad that it caused my blood pressure to soar, and I had no choice but to let my family know what was happening with me.

Remember, I shared with you that I started studying Islam, but I refused to attend the meetings because there was so much confusion within the meetings. Notwithstanding my not attending the meetings, I considered myself to be a part of the Islamic studies. Some of the captives who participated in the meetings did not feel that I should wear the hijab because I did not attend the meetings and because I sang in a Christian choir. These particular back-stabbing sisters of the nation told the loud unprofessional Villein that I was no longer a Muslim because I had not been attending the meetings.

Captives are standing in front of the doors of our assigned rooms. The Villein officer who showed favoritism to those sisters of the nation, who had alleged that I was no longer a part of Islamic studies, stops in front of me. "Take that rag off your head," she said with a smirk. "This is not a rag, I stated," but because I now understood that a captive had to follow the last command of a Villein, I removed the hijab from my head. Some captives laughed, and some looked at me with a forlorn face as I removed the hijab.

The dorm orderly, who is my bunkmate, approached me and stated, "that officer violated your religious right. You should file a grievance," noted the captive. I desired to do just that but was not sure of the process. I was informed by the Orderly that I must seek and obtain a grievance form from the very officer who I planned to grieve. I approach the officer and ask for a grievance form.

"How many do you want? Grieve me, I don't give a dam," said the Villein officer. She threw the grievance forms at me; I gather up the papers that were thrown to me. After completing the grievance form, I had to ask the same officer who I was grieving to allow me to go and see my counselor. Counselors are responsible for approving a grievance form initiated by a captive to have it move forward.

I got back to the bubble where the Villein officer is stationed. The Villein pretended she did not see me and make me wait for what seemed like 30 minutes. When she finally acknowledged me, I told her what I needed. She reluctantly called my counselor, who had an office in the same dorm. When I was finally told that I could proceed to the counselor's office, the Villein officer comes along with me. As soon as we enter the counselor's office, the Villein officer starts speaking to me in a derogatory manner. She is using profanity and sticking her finger in my face as she spews out verbal abuse. I sensed my ancestors with me, reminding me that the officer is an un-awakened one who is doing the work of the Villein lords.

I remain calm even as my instinctive mind screams to my physical self to "defend your ego," "don't take this from her, can't you see that she is lying on you, say something," but I remain composed. When the Villein has exhausted herself, I am prompted by my ancestors to turn from the Villein officer and look directly at the counselor who is a management Villein. I looked at the counselor, and very calmly explained my position. When I finished conversing on the event the way that I remembered it, the room was quiet. The counselor asks the Villein officer to step out of the office. When the Villein officer leaves, "what do you want to happen," asked the counselor. "I want to grieve that officer for violating my constitutional rights." The counselor took the grievance form from me and said that she would get back to me.

I was not aware that the counselor was supposed to provide me a receipt for accepting and signing the grievance. She had done neither. After several weeks, I received the original complaint back with a note on it that indicated I needed to sign it; however, the grievance was already previously signed by me before the counselor received it.

By the time my original grievance was returned to me, the time to grieve the incident had expired, and I had been relocated from the medical dorm of E7 to what is defined as the Honor Dorm. Understand this, filing a grievance was a process that was mandated by the system lords to protect the rights of captives; however, the constitutional rights of captives are violated every day, and there is no help anywhere to be found. Shortly after this incident, I was relocated to the Honor Dorm, or so they call it such.

Before we move on to the so-called Honor Dorm, I will complete my observation of the medical dorm. I noticed that I was having major headaches, and assumed it was because of the Villein officer screaming every day, all day. I was finally able to get a doctor's visit after completing several sick call requests. It turns out that my blood pressure was off the charts. It was so high that I was placed on a watch list and had to have my blood pressure read every day. The practitioner on duty was not a doctor. The practitioner would review my blood pressure and ask me what I was eating, but did nothing more. My blood pressure was reaching stroke conditions, and I decided that something was wrong. My daughter works in the medical field; therefore, I sent her a list of medicines that had been diagnosed for me. My daughter researched the medication and was shocked. The practitioner or someone in the medical facility had changed my original high blood medicines to a lower brand/form. You guessed it, my daughter called the slave camp and demanded that I be provided the correct medication.

When I was called back to the medical so that my prescription could be changed, I was told by the practitioner that the medicine that they had to order for me is usually used by African Americans who have challenges with high blood pressure. She said this medicine is costly. My daughter advised me that the type of medication the practitioner was referring to as being expensive was the medicine I had been prescribed prior to being sent to the prison slave camp.

CHAPTER 23

Dying to be Free

As I ponder on the number of captives that have had strokes while at this facility, I am so grateful for my Creator and for my family that fought for me to be given the correct medicine. I spoke with captives that told me they were in relatively good health when they arrived at the prison, but now they are in wheelchairs or worse. We will never hear the story of some of the captives because they died in prison of an incorrectly or undiagnosed illness. Sometimes a captive lost their life because of technicalities, such as not having access to a wheelchair.

There was a captive who I became familiar with, she cursed like a sailor, but was the sweetest person one could meet. She was preparing to go home as she was scheduled to be released from the slave camp within a week. She asked me to plait her hair. She asked me because I could plait hair well. She was so excited; I could hear her on the phone talking with her family about what she wanted to eat when she arrives home. I had occasionally witnessed on more than one occasion that she had a difficult time breathing as she and other captives walked to the dining hall. She would often stop and rest several times before she could make it up the steep hill to eat. I asked her why she did not have a wheelchair like some of the others, "I keep asking for one, but they won't approve it," she said. Not providing this individual with a wheelchair did not make any sense to me. I witnessed management lords speaking to her when she would sit and rest. They would ask her if she was alright, and would say, "I am ok, just need to catch my breath." In my mind, I realized that this captive was having a difficult time breathing; therefore, I could not understand why she was not approved for a wheelchair.

Some captives had wheelchairs and did not seem to need them. A captive who was not of color had the wheelchair assigned to her, taken away. I am not sure what she did beyond blasting the management Villein, but she was reassigned her wheelchair. I was told that this captive walked up the hill in a fast stride, picked up the wheelchair that was reassigned to her, and rode it back to the dorm. I am not saying that not being of color had anything to do with this. I am just stating what happened.

One morning I was awakened to a captive screaming out that "she is dead." I thought I was dreaming at first but suddenly realized that what I was hearing was real. Most of the captives were still locked in their rooms as it was only about 4:00 AM, but those who were given early morning medicine were released from their quarters. One of these captives did not go back to her room after taking her medicine and witnessed what happened.

I was told by the captive that witnesseth the incident, that the ambulance was called when the deceased captive began having difficulty breathing. It was also stated by other captives that the deceased captive had gone to medical earlier the previous evening complaining that she could not catch her breath, but was sent back and told to put in a sick call.

On the morning of her death, we were placed on lockdown in our rooms; however, the captive that had been outside her room told everyone what she witnessed. Later that day, when we were finally allowed to leave our rooms, the Warden came in to tell everyone what we should believe and warned us not to say anything to anybody about the occurrence. The Warden also reminded us how many times the deceased captive had been in and out of prison as if this was the cause of her death. The deceased captive's Bunkie was isolated for several hours before any other captives were able to speak with her. The Bunkie would only say that she was trying to revive the deceased captive, but could not.

It was said that the family of the deceased captive was not informed that she had transcended, and as a result, they came to pick her up as if she would be released the next week. I can't even imagine what her family must have felt. Unfortunately, her family will never know the truth of how she suffered. The is the same individual who should have had a wheelchair to travel back and forth to the dining hall, the same individual whose hair I had plaited. She would never get to eat the meal planned for her by her family, and she would never get to show off her hairstyle.

While being held captive, I was aware of captives attempting or committing suicide. Medical misdiagnoses resulted in captives having cancer throughout their body. Captives even had the incorrect tooth extracted. Captives fell and were injured as a result of being chained while being taken to outside medical appointments. Some older captives choose not to go on outside medical appointments because they were afraid they would be hurt during transport.

Unfortunately, captives who do not have family members on the outside have no voice. No one is going to call to ask questions. They die or are crippled, and the lords tell their version of the story if anyone asks, and most of the time, it's only other lords who ask the questions.

*(**The lords asking the questions and those giving the answers have a common goal. Contain the truth.**)*

Chapter 24

Prison Camp
Mental Ward or Both

I am sitting in the lobby of E7, and a captive stands up and leaps from the wheelchair that she is sitting in. She leaps and climbs to the top of a table, and she starts dancing on the top of the table, hurling profanity at everyone around her at the same time, then on top of all of this, she starts to preach all while standing on the top of the table. I did not even know the captive could walk, much less jump on the top of a table. As I sat with my mouth wide open, a captive looked at me and said, "this fool does this all the time. "It's the medicine they have her on; the show will be over in a minute." But, the show was not over, because the captive dancing on the table overheard what the captive said about her and focused her attention on this captive.

The dancing captive then jumped from the table and slapped the captive who verbally violated her lane. The captive who was hit was also in a wheelchair. She stood up and knocked the table dancing captive to the floor. I was flabbergasted, but from experience, I knew that I needed to get away from the action. I started moving closer to my assigned room, moving closer to safety. Other captives circled the scene to watch, and others screamed out to the Villein officer. The Villein would not leave the bubble that protected her from those being held captive. While the fight is occurring, other captives began to have seizures, not one captive, but multiple captives are falling to the floor. Within minutes the Cert team came in dressed in their black and took both of the captives to the lockdown. Medical followed, but they only watched the captives go through the seizures; it seems that there is not a lot that can be done when a person has a seizure.

Many captives are given powerful medicines that seem to bring on seizures, and then some are stimulated by the vibrations of negative energy or by others experiencing seizures. Regardless of what brings on a seizure, I am convinced of this truth, and that is, those who I witnessed having the majority of the seizures appeared to be captives being prescribed high dosages of mental health drugs. I observed that individuals being captured in the prison slave camp had severe psychological problems, but the root problem went untreated. The deep-rooted problems seem to encompass mental health. The solution used by the slave camp Villein seemed to be, prescribe mental health drugs and if that did not work, prescribe stronger mental health drugs so the captive would sleep and cause the Villein less trouble. Serving captives powerful medications was a common thread of control used in the prison slave camp. Now you can see why I was alerted by my ancestors not to take the mental drugs that the medical Villein recommended. The medical Villein told me that the drugs would help me to sleep. I choose to take my chances to fall asleep without drugs. It was not easy as often other captives screamed out in the night or talked very loudly, but I endured to maintain my sanity. Even if one did not have mental challenges, I have witnessed that using the prescribed drugs caused a constant desire from the usage of such medications.

(I raise this question: Why is the system placing those in prison that should, in my opinion, be cared for in a place that is better equipped to assist the individual with mental challenges. Yes, the prison has mental health counselors, but these counselors only have time to talk and prescribe mental health drugs. Rehabilitation of captives is one of the goals of prisons. However, I discovered that a prison is a place that houses too many mentally challenged individuals.)

Chapter 25

US Constitution
Amendment 13
Dressed Up As Rehabilitation

Most of the captives housed in E7 or the medical dorm or so it's called did not work because they were constrained to wheelchairs or walkers. Captives who were in good health were responsible for completing tasks like cleaning the showers and other cleaning details. I was appointed to clean the showers on our hallway by the self-appointed dorm orderly. I refer to the assignment as a detail because, in my mind, when one works, they are compensated for the work they perform. In this prison slave camp, everyone who was able worked details for no pay. The Dorm Orderly assigned me the work detail of keeping the showers cleaned on our hallway. She then told me she would perform the work if I paid for her. Payment would be the form of items purchased from the prison store. So not only would I not be paid for performing the work, but now the Dorm Orderly wanted me to pay her to do the job.

I declined the offer. The Prison camp also defined some captives as medical helpers. It was these individuals who were responsible for cleaning up after a captive missed the bathroom. I observed captives having to clean up the feces of another not being provided gloves or anything to protect their hands or nose. Captives who had been in prison slave camp for more than five years showed me their hands and indicated that the nerves in their hands were numb from placing their hands in so much bleach. I decided to ask for gloves to clean the showers as I did not want the nerves dying in my hand, and having gloves would be much more sanitary.

I go to the bubble where the officer is housed, and ask the Villein officer, "could I please have some gloves so that I may clean the shower?" We don't give out gloves, sneered the Villein, without even lifting her head to speak. "I need some gloves because the bleach is too strong for my hands," I appealed to the Villein again.

Now clearly frustrated, the Villein looks up at me. "Look, inmate, I told you that we do not give out gloves, this is a prison, you don't get to have it your way," sneered the Villein. Left with no other options, I walk away thinking that the showers are not going to get very clean today. Most captives located gloves from different sources and made them available to those of us who could afford them.

Remember, I told you that after my encounter with the loud Villein in E7, I was moved to the Honor Dorm. Well, let me fill you in on how all that occurred. While in E7, I decided that I wanted to do something more than to keep the dorm in order. Within the first week of a captive arriving at the camp, they are assessed to determine where they are going to be placed to work for free. My ancestors had communicated within me that I was to observe and learn. Before going to the classifications, which is a fancy name for a group of General

Counselors who listen and assign you to the ***"work for free" farm***, I heard other captives talk about the process of classifications. One captive said if you go into classification, not knowing who you are or what you want to do, they are going to assign you to work in the kitchen, and you will have a hard time getting out of that job. Worse, they could place you on outside grounds. Working on outside grounds is terrible because it's cold in the winter and hot in the summer. There are a lot of snakes in the ditch area when one is working on outside detail. When you are in the ditches weeding, snakes pop their heads up, and you have to cut their heads off with the weed waker, related one captive. This captive seems to speak from experience. This captive did not realize that they were giving me the roadmap that would keep me from a path of hard labor.

Before going to the classifications, I hand wrote my resume' and handed it to the counselors upon entering the room where the assessments were being held. I followed instructions given by the captives checking us in, and by the time I left the classifications, I was not a candidate for the kitchen or outside grounds. In fact, after a couple of months of being a dorm orderly in E7, I was assigned the detail in the library. In my mind, I thought I had hit the jackpot even if I was working for free. You see, I love to read, and thought the library would serve me as I served the captives who came in to check out books.

Don't start giving any high fives yet, as this was the detail from hell. The management Villein was as cruel as an alligator that swallows up an innocent victim. This Villein used every technique of the Willie Lynch System. I would not be surprised to discover her picture in the "how to make a slave serve you" section if such a section existed in a book. She divided and conquered captives. She sought to demean captives at every opportunity. I thought she did not like people of color, but I soon realized that every captive had their day to receive less inhuman treatment by the plainclothes Villein. I wondered why other captives did not congratulate me when I told them that I had been assigned to detail in the library. I thought perhaps they were jealous of my circumstance, but as I thought back, I realized they looked at me with sad eyes, and their eyes seem to say, "good luck with that."

My first day and the days and months to follow on the library detail was constant work. The first hour we would clean up, mend books, try to keep from being the mat that the Villein stepped on for the day, and then prepare for captives to arrive to check out books. The antiquated system used to keep up with what books were being checked out and whom they were being released to consisted of small index cards that were so thin that they often crumbled and sank to the bottom of the wooden box we kept them in. This process caused us to search and hunt for a captive's handwritten library card. The unsuspecting captive at the end of what we called service often left the library without being able to check out a book because their so-called library card could not be located. The management Villein would not allow the captive to check out a book if their card could not be found. One morning, the management Villein met with us and said, "If you see any improvements that you feel could make or assist in providing better service, let me know." Well, this was my area of expertise, and as well as an open door for me to discuss changes that I thought would cause the library services to operate more effectively, I thought.

I went to the Villein and pitched the concept of having me build an excel spreadsheet that would maintain the names of the captives checking out books as well as provide a book inventory. This Villein looked at me and said, "we do not use computers in here, and never will."

I assumed the Villein believed developing an excel spreadsheet would require an internet connection. I smiled and said that the system that I am recommending would not require internet access. My statement was dismissed as a bell ringing to dismiss students at the end of a school day. It was as if I had never spoken, and the meeting was ended abruptly by the management Villein. Sad to say, this was the last day that this Villein smiled at me. After that, I was screamed at for arriving at the detail 5 minutes early. I was told that I could not read a book when on break, but make no mistake about it; she treated everyone detailing in the library the same. I soon learned her treatment of captives went beyond that detail in the library, for she poured out venom on those visiting the library to check out books just as brutal. I observed that she would single out one captive that she would be kind to for perhaps a week. When she did this, I noticed that the other captives would seem to feel some way. They would seem to become jealous. Speaking for myself, I felt like I was in a scene straight out of *Roots*. The captive receiving pleasantries would most often make the mistake of believing they were on the Villein "good list" only to discover a week later that they were now on the receiving end of the harsh treatment. What an emotional roller coaster.

There was an occasion that this management Villein called me into her office. At this time, I had recently been relocated to the honor dorm, and the year is 2018. Ok, I know it took a little while to get back to the Honor Dorm, but I needed you to know more about my journey. I thought the management Villein in the library where I detailed was calling me in her office to congratulate me on my recent move to the honor dorm as this move was defined as a privileged one. Still, to my surprise, she attacked me mercilessly, ruthlessly and maliciously with verbal threats that were built around her assumptions, she said that people have been talking about the lack of customer service in the library and that I was one of the people being talked about. I realized that she was trying to transfer what she was feeling to me. After all, I was the new captive on the block, and she thought I did not know the truth. Captives in the honor dorm had already spoken about how they quit detailing in the library as they had experienced the viciousness from the same Villein as I was experiencing. I listened to captives talk about how they had grieved this Villein after being denied access to the legal library. For many other reasons, however, nothing ever happened to her by their account. Additionally, there were many captives and others that spoke highly of the excellent services received in the library from the captives. After I listened to her harsh account of untruths, I asked for permission to speak, and she allowed me to speak.

Sensing the strength of my ancestors with me, I speak. "You say people are talking about me and the others who are detailing in this library. You say people are saying that we are not providing good customer service; however, I look around, and I am the only person you called into this meeting, I am confused about your actions. I ask you; can I speak honestly with you?" She said, "yes." I continue speaking, "you may or may not know that captives don't like coming to this library because of how you treat them. They tolerate the law library because they don't have a choice. When people ask me how I can stand working/detailing for you in this library; I never say anything negative about you, there is a problem with customer service, and that problem resides with you. Not only do you treat the individuals who detail for you ruthlessly, but you are also relentless and unkind to those entering the doors hoping to experience some normalcy. I have witnessed you trying to divide and conquer the people who detail for you and even your peers. I must say that for me, I do not will the acceptance of the burden that you wish to place upon me, as it belongs to you, and you only."

After I finished speaking, she told me that I was excused from her office. The next day I reported to the detail 3 minutes early, and she told me to go back to the dorm after harshly telling me that she had a right to write me a Derogatory Report for reporting too soon. She also stated that she would call me when I could return to the detail, I was so upset; I knocked on the door of the General Counselors who shared an office inside the library. I was motioned to enter. I told the two counselors in the office of what had just occurred. They seem to know already this Villein history of mistreating captives. I asked the General Counselors to have my assigned counselor contact me as she was out that day. I also wrote a letter to my assigned counselor, asking to be released from that detail. The callous management Villein called for me to return to the detail after three days. I did report to the detail. When I arrived at the detail, I ask her if she had a moment to speak with me, she said yes.

I told her that I had asked my counselor to drop me from the library detail, as I think it would be best for all involved. She agreed. I am again assigned to the role of an Orderly, but this time it was in the Honor Dorm.

CHAPTER 26

Ancestor Intervention-The Lessons

In the prison slave camp, I learned that one must be still and observe and focus on an item or situation to gain knowledge of the item or situation entirely; therefore, I focused. It was during this time that the ancestors were directing me to read and study various books. Books such as, (1 Beyond Positive Thinking, (2 Mystic Christianity, (3 Human Aura Astral Colors & Thought Forms, (4 Yoga Sutras of Patanjali, (5 Raja Yoga, and many others. I chose the authors of these books as my mentors even though they had long ago transcended, and these mentors taught me how to train my mind and body, as well as understand the "I" within the human-self.

Settling in the Honor Dorm was easy as it was much quieter. I was able to get my study without being interrupted. After completing the trivial tasks, tasks that did not require me to place my hands in bleach and other chemicals, I had hours to research and study.

("Someone said, "If you don't want them to know something, put it in a book, they'll never read it." I am not sure who said this as my research did not reveal the author of this

statement; however, I understand it was a statement widely used during and after the desegregation of the schools.)

Unfortunately, in the prison slave camp, this statement was made more apparent to me. I thought those in the honor dorm would be more concerned with knowledge and helping other captives. I discovered that the Honor Dorm is a place within the walls of the prison slave camp that separates those who believe that they are above lower-class captives. Captives in the Honor Dorm read some non-fiction, but the majority of captives would not read anything that would enrich their mind. Most of the captives had never taken the opportunity to download books from the kiosk. Many books contained knowledge that benefited me. The electronic books were $.99 per download, and the knowledge they held remained silent, waiting to be released to any captive who stretched out their mind to it. As far as I was concerned, this knowledge was priceless.

I was taught to believe a certain way all my life. Go to school, work hard, believe Jesus will fix it after a while, and then one day, you will go to heaven. Imagine how I felt when I begin to thaw out from years of being frozen in a religious system that served itself. When I started to awaken, I wanted to awaken everybody. I told captives about the books that I had read or was reading. They started calling me "Ms. Professor." When I invited them to attend a class that I offered to the dorm regarding "choosing your thoughts," only one person attended. Captives did not seem to want to be awakened from the illusion of system imprisonment or where they are just frozen in a non-deliberate thought pattern. A pattern that had been ingrained within their mind. Their way of thinking had been taught for way too long.

Captives in the Honor Dorm were doing everything other captives did in separate dorms, but things were done within the confines of the walls of the honor dorm. However, the actions of the captives led me to perceive that their mind had led them to believe that they had arrived.

The Villein officers of the honor dorm were not as cruel as those of other dorms because there were captives that had work details in the Warden's office, and the Villein thought their offensive actions might get back to the Warden. The Honor Dorm Villein would state say that they did not welcome working in the Honor Dorm because the snitches made sure that the Warden was told everything that happens. I often wondered why it mattered what got back to the Warden, as the Warden did not seem to care about the captives. She was more concerned with perception. The Warden's illusion of the prison explains why just before the outside lords were inspecting the slave camp, captives were required to paint, buff floors, and do whatever was necessary to demonstrate that the prison was a happy and appealing place of stay. She was very concerned with the image of the Honor Dorm, as well as the image of the Faith and Character Dorm. The Faith and Character Dorm is one where captives are supposed to develop their character.

The double standard system created by the lord Villein separated the Honor Dorm and the Faith and Character Dorm from other dorms, such as E9 and E8. Dorms E8 and E9 housed the majority of the gang members and those who were defined as trouble makers. Management Villein often openly discussed E8 and E9 as if they were of a lower class of captives. I remember thinking to myself if only you knew what happens in the Honor Dorm when you are not watching.

Captives were sleeping with each other, theft, fights, arguments, and much more. The difference is, the scuttlebutt of truth is contained in the Honor Dorm, and from what I was told., the Faith and Character Dorm had the same challenges.

When a captive became brave enough to write a note to a management Villein to release the truth, the management Villein would arrive unannounced and demand that all captives report to the lobby. With all the one hundred and ninety-two captives being summoned to the lobby area of the dorm, the verbal torture would commence. Management Villein would then call out the captive who wrote the note, or look directly at the captive, saying, "I received a note stating that some of you are going in rooms that you are not assigned to." Often they would provide just enough information so that the group could ascertain who wrote the note. The group would follow the eyes of the management Villein, and then everyone would have an idea of the person who told or snitched, which is the term used in the prison camp. More than once, captives who were defined as snitches were caught in the shower area where there were no cameras. The only evidence that there was a struggle, or should I say a beat down, was a knot on the head or a black eye on the captive who snitched.

I realized that I did not want to become a part of any circle that punished you for telling the truth. I had been there and done that, nor did I plan to snitch. In my mind, a snitch is someone who throws a rock and then hides their hand. A snitch desires to see the window broken, but is a coward as they do not want to accept the consequences for breaking the window. They will allow others to shoulder the blame before they would step forward and own up to their transgressions. Therefore, when I recognized that a captive's deed would place the burden on all captives' shoulder, I would openly say to that captive responsible for the performance of the misdeed, and to all who could hear… "I am not a snitch because I am saying this in the open, I will not participate in any offenses that would cause me to be issued a disciplinary report. If I am asked who is responsible for this offense, I will say your name openly. I will not accept the responsibility for the undertaking of one."

Some of you may read the last statement above and form an opinion or allow the mind to believe it to be one of selfishness on my part but consider this. Every person is responsible for what happens to them.

(I now choose to be proactive in my responsibility to myself. I know that there is only <u>Me</u> that places <u>Me</u> in a situation, and there is only me who can change my present. And you know what? Captives respected my position and made sure that I was not a witness to any of their transgressions.)

CHAPTER 27

Path to Least Resistance is Freeing

It is a public record that I received a sentence of 50 years serve 20. Although this sentence was issued by what the system refers to as a Judge, I understand that I am the Producer, Director, and Actor of my life. The time I invested in educating myself, meditating, and listening to the guidance of my ancestors made me aware that I held the key to my freedom. Every script that was written and acted upon was through guidance. And even when a result did not meet my expectations, I had a knowing that that outcome served a higher good.

I am sitting in the honor dorm, and I am doing what I do most mornings. That is to read and meditate and seek guidance. I reflected on an instance when I was housed in the medical dorm, E7. I remember having an instant thirst for water. A craving that I had to quench right away, and since bottled water was a thing of the past for a captive, I walk to the water fountain to get a drink. I bend down to get a drink, and I am prompted to look up. There is a beautifully painted picture of a mountain hanging over the water fountain, the image is directly in my sight of view, and it was at the exact level of my head when bending to drink from the fountain. This is not typically true for me. I am 5'2," and most pictures are hung so that I must strain my neck to get a good view of them, but not this one. The image had an inscription written on it. The inscription that was written said this. ***"You Were Assigned to this Mountain so you could show everyone that this mountain could be moved."*** As I gazed at the painting, the words written seemed to pulsate toward me. The words confirmed to my personal-self what had already been revealed to my inner self. I wrote the inscription down because I never wanted to forget it.

I asked other captives if they had ever read the inscription on the picture above the water fountain, there was not one captive who said that they had ever noticed the painting or the inscription written on the painting. No one knew what painting or picture I was speaking. I then knew for sure that the universe had caused an Artist to imagine that piece of work, directed them to paint it, and place it over the water fountain for me at such a time when I would discover it.

It was in January 2019. After I had begun to soak up knowledge, the Universe wanted me to share the experience. It was not my intention to share anything. I had decided that I would gain an understanding of things for myself. It seemed to me that others were not interested. My ancestors prompted me to understand that the knowledge that had been calling to me and given to me was not only for me. It was for the oneness of all to know. So, with eagerness, I accept a work-for-free recreational aide position.

I am now detailing in the medical dorm every day. The same dorm that I was once housed. I facilitate a class that I developed from the book entitled <u>Beyond Positive Thinking</u>. As I shared my account of the painting that hung over the water fountain to the class I was facilitating, they all looked at me like a deer staring into headlights. I ask them, have you seen the painting? They respond with a resounding "No." I leave the class to go and look for the picture, and its nowhere to be found. One captive said she thinks she remembered the painting, but no one could tell me what happened to it. Even the people who still resided in the dorm after I had moved to the honor dorm did not remember what happened to the picture.

(Things come into our path for a reason. If we allow them, they will serve their purpose and then move on.)

In another chapter, I started to tell you about the illusion of the appeal attorney that we hired. We thought this attorney would help to free me. We discovered much too late that this attorney was more of the same of what we had already experienced. It took my daughter consistently calling him before he came to visit me, and when he did visit, he did not have a strategy of how he would proceed. The attorney's lack of attention and expertise may explain why the judge ruled against my appeal.

We went to court on an appeal in December of 2018. The appeal attorney came to visit me while I was in the county jail waiting to appear before the appeal judge. This was the second time that the appeal attorney had visited me, and we had hired him over two years ago. By the way, the appeal judge is the same judge who sentenced me to 50 years of servitude.

In January 2019, after the new year was in our past, my daughter told me that the judge had denied the Motion in its entirety. After learning this news regarding the court's decision, I spoke to my daughter over the phone, and said to her, *"the judge nor the DA has ever held power. We hold power in thought."* It was at this moment that it seemed that my entire mind illuminated. My physical body appeared to have a burst of an irregular heartbeat. I did not speak to my daughter about this at the time, as I did not want her to worry. However, I did realize that I must end the phone call with my daughter right away. I was glad when the system said that our time had expired on the phone, which allowed me to embrace what I was feeling. I hung up the phone and went to the room that I was assigned to, laid across the bed, and closed my eyes. I reflected on the vision of the man of tears and the strong man that I had encountered several weeks ago. I shared the vision with you in a past chapter. I sensed my ancestors rejoicing because they were witnessing my awakening to the concept and the lessons they were teaching.

I considered the judicial system as being unjust, powerful, and stronger than myself. The illusion presented to my mind is that the system always wins; however, it is the engagement of such thoughts that provided the energy necessary to cause the manifestation of the thing thought upon or about.

(The most challenging task I have ever undertaken in my entire life was to "See No Evil, Hear No Evil, Speak No Evil, and Think No Evil.")

Imagine this. The attorney we secured did not bother to contact my family or me. He forwarded the judge's decision in an email to my daughter and fled the scene. We called him after receiving the email; however, he never responded to my constant emails or calls. My ancestors revealed to me that the attorney was assigned to do just what he did because my most important lesson was to experience the fact that my deliberate thoughts are the real source of anything that manifest in my world.

I was reminded from within not to become self-absorbed. Not to become attached to the outward image that was seeking to cling to my mind. I understood through the guidance of my ancestors that it would be unwise to become preoccupied with fears, hopes, plans, and even purposes. The personal-self or mind saw the illusion of what appeared to be facts and desired to cast a different picture so that other captives would embrace me. The problem with casting a different view is that it was being cast from a place of fear. You see, captives are aware when you have gone out to the court and want to know what happened upon your return. Mainly, they want to see if you are going to be released.

The personal-self molded from egotistical thoughts desired to stand up and allow the scene to be about just self. It may have been much easier for me to ignore the illusion of still being held captive if I had been placed in another dorm after returning from the court, but I was returned to the honor dorm where captives were waiting to hear the news. In the months leading to my court appearance, I had been meditating and speaking positive affirmations and being very careful to say, speak, and feel what I desire to manifest in my world. My response to the question that was asked of me from other captives of "what happened in court," was always, *"I am waiting on my paperwork from the court, and it won't be long now."*

I could have chosen to condemn the Judge, the District Attorney, and the Justice system because of the illusion that the mind seeks to present to me, but I choose to state the reality that the inner self believed to exist already. Remembering that I am the Producer, Director, and Actor, I realized that I get to write the script regardless of the illusion presented. Therefore, I produced and starred in the movie of my life. I did not concern myself with the details of how or when, but I had a knowing that what I was thinking, feeling, and stating was more accurate than anything in the world. My thoughts and feelings were the reality I chose, and the script that I had written and willed for my life. I reflected and remembered in my vision that the strong man exhibited strength that seemed to destroy the man of tears; however, the man of tears is immortal and cannot be destroyed, is invincible, and could not be harmed. The vision given to me several weeks earlier through my ancestors provided the understanding that I needed. The man of tears continued to communicate with me through thought even after it seemed that the strong man eradicated him. The courts appeared to be the strong man, but one's thoughts are stronger.

There was an occasion that I was in deep meditation; I was prompted with a directive from within. The prompting vibrated a message ..., "send a request for Parole to the Georgia Parole Board." My family and I had developed the Parole package months ago and had been waiting on the attorney to submit it, but remember, the attorney had not contacted us after the denial of the Motion for a new trial. I believed that because I had an attorney of record, I needed to wait for the attorney to submit the package to the Parole Board. I was again reminded that the attorney had served his purpose, and the universe had aligned all else to do the same.

My belief system was based on the values resulting from being a product nurtured from the soil of the South. I was taught to give attention to the strength of the system and, through the fear, fight against this system that I feared. However, the fight rest in the minds of individuals, which resulted from the fear of being conquered and destroyed. My mind had forgotten that it could decide, and the greatest force is love.

(LOVE. I now understand that deliberate thoughts are all the fight that is needed. Joyce Meyer's book, <u>Battlefield of the Mind</u>, taught that the battle is in the mind. As my son Will would say, Please believe it!)

In the past, I was not aware that my ancestors were always there to guide me. It was after I had been awakened that I could see the truth. They taught me how to develop the use of my full mind, and woke up my spiritual concept of who I am. I was prompted to teach the lessons learned to those in the medical dorm, E7, and to anyone else who wanted to listen. Understand this, when I arrived in the prison slave camp, my thoughts were that I just wanted out and did not want to be bothered. But now, I understand that there is a higher purpose than my being captured in the prison slave camp.

I reread the book, <u>The Power</u> by Rhonda Byrne. I had read this book several years ago but did not remember one word that I had read and had not applied the concepts in my life. Reading this book caused me to understand the force and the power of love. I began to vibrate love to everyone and everything, including the Villein, their lords, and the system that I had believed sought to enslave me. Within four months after I began sharing knowledge with the medical dorm, E7, and vibrating the energy of love, many captives in E7 started to be released. Captives were beginning to become active and had ceased complaining about their surroundings and those around them. Within this same period, I received a notice that the 50 years to serve 20 years sentence that had been passed to me could no longer contain me in prison, I was being released. I would be released from the prison slave camp on May 14, 2019, after investing approximately two years and two months. Ironically, Mary 14 is the day my daughter, Timmesha, was born.

I walk out of the Pulaski prison gate that, for me, never existed to restrain me. On the contrary, the once locked gates served to awaken me from the Inside. I could see everything so much clearer.

Villeins were underpaid and overworked. They were part of a system that had evolved into a monstrous thing that could not be controlled. The system lords were not close enough to the intensity of what they had created to think that it was harmful to those who entered it or even worked within it. The truth is that no one could see that what they feared had come upon them, and the thing feared continued to grow as it was watered just as a farmer would irrigate a crop. And just like a seed planted, the thing planted was being produced after its own kind, yielding millions of descendants. Producing so many descendants until there was no longer any place to store the crop. The crop had taken over, and resources became inadequate to continue to produce such a vast and out of control crop. The established system did not install controls. The system had not understood that millions of seeds of all kinds would and could grow in the soil that was perhaps cultivated for a particular seed.

Villeins understood as they could see up close what the system was producing, but not being aware they could vibrate a change to the thing they no longer desired to be a part. Because they were under the illusion of being subject to their lords, they remained fastened to the system. Some Villein, who became awakened, decided they no longer wanted to produce for the system even for money, and they left the fields. Yet others used the system to benefit their lust; however, the majority moved from camp to camp, self-absorbed in the belief that each camp would be different. Sometimes the Villein and those who had been in captivity even returned to the field they recently fled, just as a dog would return to its bile, not reasoning within their mind that it is the same retch that they not long ago expelled. The difference, however, is that the dog has not a mind to reason. Humans, on the other hand, do possess this ability. The ability must be awakened within.

I understood that it was not just those wearing the brown uniforms that were captured. It was also those who were subject to the system that was also in captivity. This is what my ancestors taught me in the vision of the man of tears and the strong man. The stronger one is the one who uses the power of the enlightened and deliberate mind, not just physical strength.

My Takeaway

I realized one remains a captive when the illusion of captivity is the conscious thought. When one is awakened, then they can free themselves. When I understood that it is me, the real me and that I have always been responsible for what happens to me, "I Screamed From The Inside." You see, I believed in a divine intervention outside of myself. Spending time with me taught me that I must trust what is within and that looking for an external savior is no longer an option for me.

In my next book, "Awaken Within" I will share much more on how I was awakened from the inside.

Thank you, reader, for reading my story. The accounts in this book are real. Names were changed to protect the identity of the people involved.

All the information contained in this book are true and the personal experience of the author. The mentioning of any other author does not constitute an infringement on any author's copyright.

www.ingramcontent.com/pod-product-compliance
Lightning Source LLC
Chambersburg PA
CBHW021952290426
44108CB00012B/1034